RIVER EFFRA

'We have not only destroyed the former beauty of South London: we have forgotten it.'
Walter Besant, 1898

RIVER EFFRA

SOUTH LONDON'S
SECRET SPINE

JON NEWMAN

Signal

First published in 2016 by
Signal Books Limited
36 Minster Road
Oxford
OX4 1LY
www.signalbooks.co.uk

A catalogue record for this book is available from the British Library.

ISBN 978-1-909930-42-1 Paper

Production: Tora Kelly
Cover Design: David Western
Cover Images: David Western
Printed in India

CONTENTS

PREFACE

Every day thousands of people cross the River Effra. London buses travelling south over Vauxhall Bridge pass by its mouth, main line passengers heading into Waterloo cross it at Vauxhall, while suburban trains waiting outside Herne Hill and West Norwood stations straddle it; the Northern line at Oval burrows beneath it and cars on the A23 at Brixton Road hug its valley. Yet the drinkers in the Half Moon at Herne Hill no longer hear its flow beneath the cellars, the commuters descending from the Victoria line at Brixton no longer sense the weight of its water above their heads, nor do the mourners in Norwood Cemetery spy its ghost passing among the headstones. For the Effra has vanished.

It is not the only London river to have been tidied away underground, but somehow its vanishing feels more complete. The River Fleet still murmurs on Hampstead Heath in the Hampstead and Highgate Ponds and its valley beneath Holborn Viaduct is still in plain sight. The Westbourne can be guessed at in the Serpentine and is almost tangible in its pipe above the station platform at Sloane Square Tube. In South London the Wandle, the Graveney, the Ravensbourne and the Quaggy are yet above ground, while the mouths of the Neckinger and the Falcon Brook can be seen at St Saviour's Dock in Southwark and as a patch of ornamental planting amid the show towers of Battersea's waterfront. Of the Effra virtually nothing remains.

There is something about an underground river that trumps all the other *subterranea* out there. Deep shelters, gas mains, disused Tube tunnels and cable ducts have their charms for some, but these are the latter-day products of an infrastructure-clogged age, whereas a river lives on in the mind as something primordial and pre-societal. Does that explain why so much has been written on the Effra, and why such an attentive fraternity of local historians, cryptopotamophiles, dowsers, *flâneurs*, urban explorers, geologists and metropolitan mythographers continue to revisit it?

In joining this throng I have tried to create a comprehensive work, one that considers the pre-, medieval and early-modern history of the river as well as that more familiar 'vanishing point' in the nineteenth century when the Effra was sacrificed by the Metropolitan Board of Works on the altars of civil engineering and public health. I have tried as well to tease out some of the urban myths that have clotted around it—to separate out the 'psycho' from the -geographer without destroying the allure that this small underground stream in South London undoubtedly still possesses.

Many people have been extremely generous with their time and their knowledge. I would particularly like to thank two people: Martin Knight for his expert understanding and explanation of the geology and geography of the Effra basin; and Graham Dawson for kindly sharing his research into the medieval court records that shed light on the earlier course of the river. Any lingering solecisms in these areas are of my transmission, not their commission. Thanks also for their advice on many particular and different aspects must go to Keith Bailey,

John Brunton, Jeff Doorn, Colin Fenn, Bob Flanagan, Laurence Gomme, Stephen Humphrey, Peter Jefferson Smith, Gareth King, Ian McInnes, Helen Spring and Alun and Barbara Thomas. I must also thank Jane Hartwell of Morley Gallery who hosted the *Water Lambeth* exhibition which I curated in 2015 and which was the starting point for this book.

I owe an enormous debt to the archives and record offices of London and in particular to two collections: those held by Lambeth Archives and those of the London Metropolitan Archives. Without access to these records this book would have remained almost as dark and unilluminated as the Effra in its sewer.

Finally I want to thank David Western, artist, friend and fellow traveller who has accompanied me on field work trips along the Effra over the last two years. The journeys were always made on push bikes—sadly the red Chevrolet Caprice convertible was unavailable—and concluded in one of South London's dwindling number of pubs. I thank him for his company, his excellent maps and the photographs that illustrate the book.

ACKNOWLEDGEMENTS

All historic images are reproduced from the collections held by Lambeth Archives Department. All contemporary photographs and maps are the work and copyright of David Western, with the following exceptions: p. 8, The Brixton Heron, Maggi Hambling, 2010, photo by Claire Peg; Plate 8B, Rosendale allotments 2015, photo by London Wildlife Trust.

ABBREVIATIONS
LAD   Lambeth Archives Department
LMA   London Metropolitan Archives
TNA   The National Archives

1

THE LIE OF THE LAND

Many things about a river which first appear innate are actually imposed. Decisions about name, the precise location of its source, its surface landscape, what is the main stream and which are the tributaries—these are not immutable facts but are all the result of human decisions or human interventions. When a river like the Effra gets put under ground and diverted into new channels then something as seemingly fundamental as its course gets called into question. By contrast, the underlying geology and geography that shape and give rise, so to speak, to the river are relatively stable, almost non-negotiable, and this chapter will consider these.

It is not possible to talk about the geology of the Effra without considering the larger geology of the underlying Thames basin. From the encircling hills to the north, south and west of London, many small streams rise and flow down to drain into the Thames. Its basin has an underlying base of chalk covered by sedimentary layers of what were once coastal sands and gravels and overlaid in turn with offshore muds; it is this which has become the London Clay, a thick deposit which extends across the Thames basin. The Effra drains a small part of the southern limb of the downfold of the Thames basin, meaning that the basin is tilted and so to the south the chalk is exposed along the North Downs. In the central area of Greater London this upper clay layer is many hundreds of feet thick.

The river we now call the Thames and which flows through this basin to its estuary is relatively recent in geological terms, having only settled into its current course in the late stages of the last Ice Age around 10,000 years ago. This was during the transition from the Pleistocene to the Holocene periods, a post-glacial moment when the decay of the ice-sheets was creating a warmer climate and higher sea levels. Archaeologists now understand that the Thames here would have been a wider multi-channelled stream extending south of its present course across north Southwark and Lambeth. This 'braided' river had multiple parallel channels with many eyots or small islands, mudflats and back waters. The Thames did not assume a single deeper channel until 4000-3000 BC. By then de-glaciation had led to a rise in sea levels which increased the tidal reach of the Thames and changed its flood plain.[1] Into this shifting riverscape the Effra and other tributaries descended from the circle of hills to pick their way to the sea.

By around 2000 BC the raised sandy eyots from which the Thames had retreated in Southwark and Lambeth began to be settled and cultivated. But even by that date it is difficult

---

1   *The Prehistory and Topography of Southwark and Lambeth*, MOLAS Monograph 14, 2002

to talk about a fixed course for the Effra through the marshes of the south bank into the Thames. At Nine Elms, Vauxhall, Lambeth, Southwark, Bermondsey and Rotherhithe a multiplicity of watercourses, many little more than ditches, found their way through the low-lying lands to the river, only gradually becoming formalised into more permanent networks of, sometimes man-made or man-modified, dykes and sluices that later still acquired names: the Heathwall, the Duffield, the Earle, the Lock and the Neckinger.

London Clay is the immediate bedrock underlying the Effra basin. While it remains underground it is a stiff bluish-grey clay, but on exposure it weathers down to a pale yellowish brown colour and becomes darker brown where soils have formed on it. Its fine-grained particles become heavy and cloying when saturated and are highly impermeable. Because it is soft and erodes easily, it is generally only found at lower levels but unusually here it is found at heights above three hundred feet along the ridge of hills at Crystal Palace and Upper Norwood, partly because of a gravel capping that protects the clay. It is the effect of rainwater percolating through this gravel down to the water table of impermeable clay beneath that has formed the line of springs found in these hills which give rise to the Effra's many streams.

The Effra's basin is a rectangle of about eight square miles and no more than six miles in length; it is bounded at its southern and south-eastern watershed by a steep, narrow two-mile ridge of hills that extends from Crystal Palace and Upper Norwood along Sydenham Hill to Westwood Park, just into Lewisham. A northward-projecting spur from the Norwood Ridge, running from Streatham Common and through Brixton Hill, separates the Effra from the River Wandle and its tributaries to the west. The Ravensbourne basin lies to the east of the Effra on the down slope of Forest Hill and Westwood Park. Within the basin of the Effra its headwaters once gave rise to many minor streams including those at Streatham Hill, Beulah Spa, Sydenham Hill, Dulwich Woods, Peckarmans Wood, Horniman Gardens and Westwood Park. Many of these higher streams are still visible, particularly after heavy rain, and one of them flowing down Sydenham Hill even has a name: the Ambrook (see Plate 1).[2] However, this book will focus on the main stream of the Effra and its two main branches: the Upper Norwood and the Lower Norwood (see Plates 2 and 3).

These two streams rise just under half a mile from one another on the steep, narrow ridge of the Norwood hills; the upper branch from beneath the site of the Crystal Palace High Level Station and the lower branch in Westow Park. They are kept apart by another ridge running north from the main line of hills to the high ground of Norwood Cemetery—and named at various points along the way as Salters Hill, Auckland Hill and Pilgrims Hill. This 'interfluve' keeps the two streams separate until they join just to the north of the South Circular Road.

In historic landscape terms both these streams rose within what was until 1806 the Great North Wood. They descended their steep hills through the oak woodlands of the Archbishops of Canterbury. A survey of 1647 found that the three hundred acres of Lambeth woodland within the Great North Wood contained some 6,300 trees, mostly pollard oaks lopped every

---

2   For more detail on the micro-geology of the Effra basin see Martin Knight's website, http://www.martindknight.co.uk/MKsResearch.html

thirty years, as well as enclosed coppices (Elder Hole on Salters Hill and Cleyland on Gipsy Hill) which were felled in rotation every ten years. As the Lower Norwood stream descended, it marked the landscape boundary between this dense managed woodland to the east and the poor grass of the 'waste' of Norwood Common to the west (through what is now Norwood Park) before flattening out to flow through the edge of what is now Norwood Cemetery and then snaking north-east across a shallow valley of water meadows to join the Upper Norwood stream at Thurlow Park Road.

The Upper Norwood stream rose adjacent to the Vicar's Oak, an ancient boundary marker that stood on the high point at the meeting point of five parishes: Lambeth, Camberwell, Penge, Bromley and Croydon. In descending Gipsy Hill the stream also defined the Lambeth and Camberwell parish boundary, slowing as it came off the slope to flow north along the line of South Croxted Road to meet the Lower Norwood stream.

Deflected by the slope of Knights Hill, the river made a long rambling loop north-east through Dulwich and back along Half Moon Lane looking for the gap in the circle of hills in order to reach the Thames. Passing through the Herne Hill gap it turned north-west to create and follow the valley between Herne Hill/Denmark Hill to the north and Knights Hill to the south that led to Brixton (See Plate 6B).

After crossing Coldharbour Lane the Effra curved through Brixton to Brixton Road at the point where the police station now stands. From here it turned north to Kennington. This stretch of the Effra must have been the earliest to be managed; when in the second century a Roman road, now the Brixton Road, was laid alongside it, the vagaries of the stream would have been tidied into a straight line (See Plate 6A).

The flat 'strong' clay lands along either side of the Effra between Kennington and Brixton were dominated by agriculture, first as farms and later, with their easy access to London's stable manure, as intensively fertilised and irrigated market gardens. The cultivation of cabbages was 'confined almost entirely to the market and farming gardeners and to the cow-keepers of Camberwell, Lambeth and Wandsworth',[3] but the area also developed a reputation for Covent Garden cash crops such as rhubarb, strawberries and asparagus.

Within the otherwise flat landscape at the north end of Brixton Road at Kennington Common stood a low mound. The Effra flowing up the line of Brixton Road was presented with a choice of routes either side of it. The evidence for the existence of an older pre-medieval course of the river flowing north-east of the mound towards Walworth will be explored later. For the moment the Effra makes an unusual right-angled turn to flow due west, passing south of St Mark's Church and then beneath Clapham Road towards The Oval.

Just occasionally along the way one gets a sense of the earlier ecology of the river. In 1570 two Kennington landholders were tasked with cutting up 'alle willows, blackthorn and brambles standing and growinge now upon the bancke of the saide sewer'.[4] In 1575 Widow Norton farming lands on Clapham Road was instructed to 'shere the banks of her shewer

---

3   *General view of the agriculture of the County of Surrey*, James and Malcolm, 1794
4   London County Council, *Court Minutes of the Surrey and Kent Sewers Commission*, vol. 1, 1909, p.178

cutting up the wethhes ther gowinge … and that she stake, wattle and wrethe the utterside of her shewer against the highe waye'. These entries from the Commissioners of Sewers' minutes give glimpses of an overgrown willow-clogged stream, as well as the practical uses that this willow (as withies) could be put to.[5] By contrast a seventeenth-century writer like John Aubrey was more interested in the medicinal herbs to be found growing alongside it. 'In the ditches about South Lambeth our *Lady's Thistle* grows frequently. But all along from hence to Kingston towards the *Thames* Side, is the greatest abundance *All-Feed* that ever I saw.'[6] (All-Feed, *Linum Radiola*, is a species of flax; Lady's Thistle is Milk Thistle.)

Beyond the Oval and approaching Vauxhall the stream was now in the alluvial flatlands of the Thames. Even in the 1780s this area was 'chiefly a marsh, and although producing a noxious vegetation from its stagnant pools, had been let for grazing'.[7] The Effra's course here is unusual, with straight lines and right-angle bends that once created field-boundaries and now run along the lines of roads, suggesting a riverscape modified by man for drainage and for boundary purposes.

The stream passed under the Wandsworth Road where it is described in 1569 as passing 'through the valley or *slade* from the bridge there called the stone bridge unto the Thames in Lambeth'; slade is an unusual Old Norse word for 'an open area of grassland or marsh between two banks' and gives us a futher sense of the low-lying geography here.[8] The stream then widened into Vauxhall Creek, enlarged through the eighteenth and early nineteenth centuries as a dock, before it flowed into the Thames just south of the present Vauxhall Bridge (See Plate 4A).

In a course of barely seven miles it had descended less than 350 feet from its sources in the Norwood Hills. At Norwood Common its stream was barely three feet wide; by Brixton it had expanded to twelve feet across, while along South Lambeth Road it was remembered as having 'the proportions of a river, wide and deep enough to bear large barges'. At its mouth as it joined the Thames it was 25 feet wide.

Small or otherwise, the Effra would have been a source of drinking water. Long after Lambeth had developed and the lower river had become polluted the upper reaches would still have been used as a local supply, certainly until the 1850s, and the nuns at Virgo Fidelis Convent

---

5   London County Council, *Court Minutes of the Surrey and Kent Sewers Commission*, vol. 1, 1909, p. 224
6   *Natural History and Antiquities of the County of Surrey*, John Aubrey, begun in 1673
7   *History of the County of Surrey*, E. Brayley, vol. III, 1847, p. 363
8   London County Council, *Court Minutes of the Surrey and Kent Sewers Commission*, vol. 1, 1909, p. 50

are believed to have continued to use the stream after that.[9] South London's private water companies initially abstracted their supply from the Thames. But in 1804 the South London Waterworks came up with a scheme for taking water from the Effra at Vauxhall Creek, pumping it to a settling reservoir at Kennington and then piping it to its customers (See Plate 4B). Time was not on the South London's side. By 1835 an angry constituent on South Lambeth Road was writing to his MP to complain that the company's channels were silted up and that the Effra, its source of supply, 'is become the receptacle of all the drains and privies of the houses on its banks from whence accumulates a quantity of feculent mud that is most pestilential and disgusting'.[10] The works were dismantled in 1847.

River water, whether feculent or clear, was not the only source of supply in the Effra basin. Cleaner, safer, medicinal and with considerably more potential for commercial exploitation were those waters to be obtained from the wells within the hills at the southern edge of the basin and which derived from the same geological source as the Effra's springs. Wells had been found and developed at Dulwich, Sydenham and at Beulah Spa and were commercially active from the seventeenth century until the 1850s.

Drawn from Nature & on Stone by T. M. Baynes.   *Printed by. C. Hullmandel.*

THE SPRING WELL CLAPHAM COMMON.

The spring well at Clapham, an example of early commercial well water extraction, ca 1820.

---

9   *Springs, Streams and Spas of London*, A.S. Foord, 1910
10 Tennyson D'Eyncourt papers, IV/3/35 (LAD)

Dulwich Wells were in the grounds of what is now the Grove Tavern on Lordship Lane; they were discovered in 1614 'at the foot of a heavy claiy hill, about 12 in number, standing together'.[11] Sydenham Wells, now Sydenham Wells Park, were active in the eighteenth century, while Beulah Spa, a latecomer developed at Spa Road in the 1830s, was passingly famous before being put out of business by the greater attractions of the Crystal Palace in the 1850s.

All three of those Effra basin wells were described as 'chalybeate', meaning that the water was strongly impregnated with iron salts. Magnesium was the other predominant mineral, as the scientist Michael Faraday discovered when he analysed Beulah Spa's waters in the 1840s. Iron and magnesium are there in such concentrations because they are direct by-products of the chemical weathering of London Clay.

Like their more famous competitors at Tunbridge and Epsom, the Effra basin waters were valued more for their medicinal than their thirst-quenching qualities. The chemically rich waters had an unpleasant taste (Dulwich water was so 'strong' that it was capable of 'piercing Tobacco Pipe clay and rendering it glassy within like China ware'[12]) and all of them were advertised as addressing an extraordinary range of medical conditions (including gout, kidney disease and skin ailments). As well as providing Londoners with a semi-rural destination for 'taking' the waters, their bottled products were widely available and supplied to London hospitals.

Fishing in the Thames at Lambeth is well-documented. The remains of an Iron Age fish trap made from wooden stakes was recently excavated on the Vauxhall foreshore while an eleventh-century custom of the manor of Lambeth required the tenant to pay an annual rental of 'half-a-thousand lampreys', a delicacy then to be found in Lambeth's marshy waters. In 1667 Samuel Pepys even saw a rare sturgeon that had been caught in the river between Lambeth and Westminster. Despite the growth in population and pollution Lambeth retained a residual fishing industry and even after the construction of London's main drainage in the 1860s flounders were being caught at Westminster Bridge.

Clearly the Effra had fish in it, but it was too small a stream to be commercially fished and there is scant evidence of its species. The Thames had long been a salmon river; Magna Carta in 1215 contained a clause requiring that all salmon weirs be removed from the Thames and, prior to their reintroduction in the 1970s, salmon had lived in the Thames and its tributaries until the 1830s. A large salmon had been caught in another tributary of the Thames at Rotherhithe as late as 1815. So that while there are no extant descriptions of salmon leaping up the Effra through Brixton and Herne Hill to spawn and die in the upper tributaries of Norwood and Dulwich, it is certainly probable that they once did.

Certainly there is evidence for that other great English migratory river fish, the eel, surviving in the upper Effra late into the nineteenth century. In 1891 the local press reported on an enormous specimen that had been found in a pond at Dulwich. After it was caught

---

11   *Natural History of the Mineral Waters in Great Britain*, Benjamin Allen, 1691
12   *Ibid*

and killed it was found, 'it measured 3 ft. 9 in. in length, was 11 in. round at the thickest point and weighed 9lb'.[13] The pond's precise location was not given, but given the eel's migratory breeding pattern, this specimen's unusual size, and therefore its likely age, it is quite plausible that it had ascended the Effra up to Dulwich before the upper river had become separated from the Thames by the London main drainage works in the 1860s and then become marooned there.[14]

The Effra had begun to be covered over in the 1820s and had completely disappeared by 1865, which meant that it vanished just before nature writers like Richard Jefferies started documenting the wild life and ecology of London. As a result there is nothing on the Effra to compare with John Ruskin's purple description of the Wandle at Carshalton in 1871, 'cutting itself a radiant channel down to the gravel; through warp of feathery weeds, all waving, which it traverses with its deep threads of clearness … starred here and there with white grenouillette [Frogbit]'; nor anything like Henry Williamson's lament for the scarred upper reaches of the Ravensbourne with, 'Snipe rising up with a cry like 'sceap!' from that hurt country - the yellow houses stretching out across fields abandoned to desolation.'[15]

Most nineteenth-century commentators on the Effra had been more preoccupied with its pollution than its wild life. It is only after it has been safely buried that the rose-tinted memories of elderly men recalling the stream of their youth began to surface. Charles Woolley, writing in 1911 remembered it at South Lambeth Road in the 1850s 'bordered up to within a few yards of what is now Vauxhall Station by bright green meadow grass banks framed with rushes as green as grass'.[16] Walter Besant, writing in the 1890s ostensibly of his schooldays at Stockwell Grammar School in the 1840s, recovers an impossible rural idyll. 'Rustic cottages stood on the other side of the stream, with flowering shrubs—lilac, laburnum, and hawthorn—on the bank, and beds of the simpler flowers in the summer; the gardens and the cottages were approached by little wooden bridges, each provided with a simple rail, painted green.'[17]

A Norwood ornithologist writing in the 1880s spoke to the 'the oldest inhabitant' who remembered a small heronry in the old Norwood woods earlier in the century and seeing 'their nests … as large as bushes, at the tops of the trees, with the birds' long legs hanging down like sticks of sealing wax'.[18] Meanwhile, another old man whose memories were published in 1912 recalled the common at Gipsy Hill in the 1850s where the Effra flowed as 'rugged in surface but bright in spring and summer with the flowers of coltsfoot, ragwort and sprays of furze blossom'.[19]

---

13   *The Echo*,16 January 1891
14   Amphibia and small fish are still found in the Effra's upper reaches along the Ambrook, and in Dulwich and Belair Park Lakes, and the Mill pond.
15   *Crown of Wild Olive,* John Ruskin, 1871; *A Test to Destruction*, Henry Williamson, 1960
16   Charles Woolley papers, ca 1911, IV/88/3, (LAD),
17   'South London of To-Day', *Pall Mall Magazine*, vol. XVI, 1898
18   *The Wild Birds of Norwood*, W. Aldridge, 1885. Herons still visit the remaining ponds, ditches and open waters of the Effra basin at Dulwich and Sydenham Hill.
19   *Norwood in Days of Old*, W.T. Philips, 1912

The Brixton Heron, by Maggi Hambling, 2010, stands above the former
Prince of Wales pub on Brixton Road and celebrates the proximity of
the Effra. While there is no evidence for a heronry in Brixton, the birds
certainly lived upriver.

Just as London's nature writers missed out on the Effra so, by and large, did London's
photographers; the river's vanishing act just pre-dated the growing affordability and portability
of cameras. One exception was William Strudwick who managed to capture its dried out river
bed at Norwood with its water meadows still edged with willows. The photo was taken in
1870, just after the Effra's stream had gone underground and just before the streets between
Lancaster Avenue and Rosendale Road were built across its valley.

The course of the Effra at Norwood with the cemetery in the background, ca 1870.

2

CUTS, COURTS AND COMMISSIONS

Look at the map of the course of the Effra (Plates 2 and 3) and there is something puzzling about the final section of its course beyond Kennington. The natural relief of the Thames basin means that South London's streams flow from south to north. The Effra complies until it gets to Kennington, where it makes a dramatic left turn to flow west to Vauxhall. From this point its progress becomes like the movement of a knight across a chessboard: a series of right-angled turns which suggest a man-made sluice or dyke. Its entry into the Thames at Vauxhall at right-angles to the river is also unusual given the natural tendency for tributaries to become 'swept downstream' and join a main river at a shallower angle. Finally one might have expected the Effra to have run towards the east here (like the other streams in the Lambeth and North Southwark promontory) to join the Thames further downstream. These oddities in its course appear to defy geography and have led to speculation that the section between Kennington and Vauxhall may be a man-made channel.

The first person to suggest this was an engineer, Thomas Codrington, who in 1915 after comparing spot heights with tidal high water points concluded that at Kennington 'an artificial channel was evidently made to divert the waters of the Effra from the marshes when the tides were shut out by the river and the embankment', but he was unable to suggest the route of its earlier course.[1]

The evidence for the possible prior course of the river is bound up with the medieval road bridges over the Effra.[2] In medieval Britain there was no central responsibility for infrastructure and the construction and the subsequent maintenance of bridges over rivers—even over one as slight as the Effra—was an expensive undertaking borne by townships or local landowners. Because of this expense it was frequently contested at law, as in a case heard at the royal court of the Kings Bench at Easter 1350. Bermondsey Abbey (also known as Bermondsey Priory) was in dispute over the maintenance of the Estbrigge (latterly Hazard's Bridge over the Effra at Brixton Road). Four local townships, Lambeth & Stockwell, Clapham, Streatham and Battersea, claimed that Bermondsey was responsible for repairing this bridge (rather than themselves) because 'in ancient times' the Abbey had obtained permission from them and from the Archbishop of Canterbury

---

1   'London South of the Thames', *Surrey Archaeological Collections*, 28, 1915. See also *River Effra*, J. Warbis, 1979, 'an archaeological assessment of potential for excavation', unpublished paper (LAD)

2   Recent research by Graham Dawson explores the issue further, *Southwark and Lambeth Archaeological Society Newsletter*, no. 133, 2015

(who held the manors of Kennington and Vauxhall) to divert the river, which must have originally flowed from Kennington north-east towards Bermondsey, into a new course. This had been done by the Abbey so that the Effra would no longer flood its lands. Because of this act, Bermondsey was now held to be responsible for the ongoing upkeep of the new bridge which it had built in order that the Effra, running along the east side of Brixton Road, could flow west under it to the Thames at Vauxhall.[3] This is the explanation for the puzzling right-angle bend.

The parties in this case are more interesting than the outcome (the litigation would drag on unresolved for decades). Bermondsey Abbey lay several miles north-east of Kennington on a small eyot of land above the tide line (Abbey Street SE1 marks the site). It also held the low-lying manors of Bermondsey and Rotherhithe whose fields were vulnerable to flooding both from the streams draining through them and from breaches of the Thames wall. Bermondsey's lands suffered from multiple inundations in the thirteenth century including the hugely damaging 'great breach of Rotherhithe' in 1294 when 'the surrounding lands of the priory were submerged' and when a commission *de Wallis et Fossatis* (walls and ditches) was appointed to review and repair the damage caused by the *refluxus ac inundaciones aquarum* (flow and flood of the waters).

Medieval religious houses like Bermondsey were powerful bodies whose wealth derived from their agricultural landholdings. Such lands became unproductive when they were flooded and clearly Bermondsey's motive for diverting the Effra was to mitigate the physical and economic risks to its assets. There are other London instances of religious houses diverting streams: the Heathwall Sluice which bounded Battersea and Lambeth at Nine Elms appears to be another man-made relief channel, possibly constructed by Westminster Abbey, to reduce the flooding of the common fields in Clapham caused by the Falcon Brook.[4]

The diversion of the Effra, while undoubtedly quite an undertaking, was probably not quite such a large piece of engineering as first appears. Dozens of sluggish dykes and sluices threaded the marshy flatness of North Lambeth and Southwark, slowly and ineffectively draining the waterlogged land, so the new course probably piggybacked on existing ditches and almost certainly joined up with an established inlet from the Thames at Vauxhall Creek. This much is suggested by another court case in 1371 about maintaining sections of the new cut. It found that Bermondsey was responsible only for the stretch west from Brixton Road as far as a point called Oldlands, where it joined up with an existing 'common ditch' already flowing into the Thames and defining the manorial boundary between Vauxhall and Kennington.[5] The litigation suggests that the new cut must have made use of existing watercourses because Bermondsey was found

---

3   KB27/259 rex m50 (TNA) and published in extenso with summaries in English in *Public Works in Mediaeval Law*, Flower, Selden Society, 1928. The other two bridges that the new cut necessitated (Merton Bridge carrying Clapham Road at Kennington and Cox's Bridge carrying Wandsworth Road at Vauxhall) were respectively the responsibility of Merton Abbey and the Abbot of Westminster.

4   *The Lost Rivers of London*, Nicholas Barton, 1962, p. 58

5   This would have been at the right-angle bend of the course at Bedser Close, SE11, where prior to ca 1700 the river split into two channels.

liable only for the first stretch, The 'common ditch' must have predated the diversion and was therefore someone else's responsibility.[6]

As for the course of the old stream, there are two candidates. The first is a more northerly gently curving course that would link it up with the Lock stream at Newington, known tributaries of which descended as far south as Kennington Lane and could have linked up with the Effra. The Lock stream passes close by Bermondsey Abbey itself, rather than its lands, and passes into the Thames via a stream of the Neckinger. While this may feel more plausible geographically, the evidence of other court records, however, suggests that the course was more likely to have taken an equally abrupt turn to the east to join up with the Earl's Sluice by flowing east across the Walworth-Camberwell Road to the bridge of St Thomas Watering at the Old Kent Road and then on to enter the Thames just south of Rotherhithe.

This is supported by evidence that long after the new cut was made, Bermondsey continued to be responsible for stretches of an older stream bed that remained 'in water' to the north-east of the diversion at Kennington. So there are court cases upholding Bermondsey's responsibility for repairing Bekwellstandard Bridge on the Walworth Road[7] and a century later in 1464 the Abbey was again held responsible for cleansing the stream known as 'le comenflodyche' east of the Old Kent Road bridge.[8] This easterly route is also supported by the later drying out of Hazard's Marsh and Walworth Marsh which lay between the Effra at Kennington and the Earl's Sluice at Old Kent Road, suggesting that the diversion at Kennington had been successful in draining these areas through which, presumably, the earlier course of the river had once flowed.

If the Earl's Sluice is indeed the original route that the Effra took to the Thames, then it must have flowed from Kennington to Walworth through Hazard's Marsh (to the east of Kennington Common/Park) and on through Walworth Marsh, latterly Walworth Common, to its east to reach the Walworth Road. Beyond the Beckwellstandard or Walworth Bridge, the course of the stream was fed by other watercourses descending from the south and remained in water as it ran east defining the parish and manorial boundary between Newington and Camberwell (along the line of what would become Albany Road) as far as the Old Kent Road where it passed under St Thomas Watering Bridge (by the Thomas A Becket pub). From this point it became known as the Earl's Sluice and flowed east, marking the parish and manorial boundaries between Camberwell to the south and Bermondsey and Rotherhithe to the north (along the line of Rolls Road and crossing Rotherhithe New Road to pass beneath the railway at Bermondsey South station, from where it still defines the present Lewisham, Southwark borough boundary and the ancient Surrey, Kent county boundary) to flow beneath another road bridge at Lower Road and enter the Thames just south of Greenland Dock.

It may be that the error lies in our modern assumption, expectation even, that there would

---

6   KB27/443/rex f20, 1371 (TNA). Bermondsey was responsible for the ditch from Estbrigge (Brixton Road) to Eldlond; the Prince of Wales, holding Vauxhall manor, for the section from Eldlond to Cox's Bridge (Wandsworth Road); and the Abbot of Westminster for the final stretch to the Thames.
7   KB27/442 rex m10 (TNA) and Selden Soc., *Ibid*
8   KB27/913 rex m6 (TNA); and *Surrey Archaeological Collections*, vol. 31, p. 137

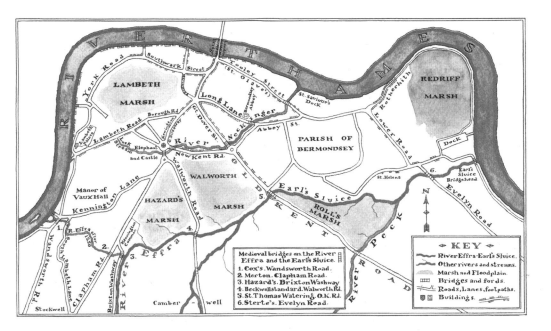

A plan showing the probable original course of the River Effra prior to the digging of the cut to the Thames at Vauxhall in the thirteenth century.

only have ever been a single course of the river. The sodden and flooded sponge of medieval Lambeth and Southwark through which the Effra moved invited the possibility of multiple exits into the Thames. It is also plausible that the new cut would have been built initially as a relief channel rather than a complete diversion and that several courses remained in water for a period until the Vauxhall route became the default and the stream through Hazard's Marsh and Walworth Marsh dried away.[9]

One gets a later glimpse of this fluid and shifting landscape in a letter written by Dr John Wallis to Samuel Pepys in 1699 recalling a walk he had made with a friend fifty years earlier from Rotherhithe across the fields to Lambeth, perhaps along the line of the Earl's Sluice. On the way they saw 'divers remains of the old channel, which had heretofore been made from Redriff to Lambeth, for diverting the Thames whilst London bridge was building, all in a straight line, or near it, but with great intervals, which had been long since filled up... People in those marshes would be more fond of so much meadow grounds, than to let those lakes remain unfilled; and he told me of many other such remains, which had been within his memory, but were then filled up.'[10]

---

9   Certainly a single puzzling naming of the Effra at Vauxhall Creek by the Commissioners of sewers in the 1560s as 'The Winterbourne ditch' might suggest that it may have only had a seasonal flow at that date.

10   *The History and Antiquities of London, Westminster, Southwark, and Parts Adjacent*, Thomas Allen, London, 1837, pp. 44-5

It is a precarious business 'divining' old watercourses. Because the early manorial court records, which would have documented the minutiae of negotiations between neighbouring manors and landholders when the new cut was being constructed, have often not survived and because the annals of Bermondsey Abbey compiled in the fifteenth century make no mention of it, the clues occur only when, rather at random, a particular dispute is taken to a higher royal court for which the records do survive. The effect is like watching a play in the dark during a thunderstorm with scraps of action caught in the flashes of lightning. What does emerge from the intermittent and sometimes conflicting evidence is that at some point after 1197 (when Canterbury acquired Vauxhall manor) and before 1350 (when its construction was being described as 'in ancient times') Bermondsey Abbey had the Effra diverted into its present course from Kennington to Vauxhall to reduce the flooding of its lands.

This profusion of litigation over the Effra and its bridges is a reminder that in the medieval period there was no single administrative or governmental body responsible for infrastructure. Disputes about rivers, roads and bridges could only be settled cumbersomely and expensively through legal actions. A landowner's 'riparian rights' and responsibilities under Common Law included the right to a flow from a watercourse passing through one's land as well as liability for neglect if one prevented that same flow from passing on to landholders downstream. Landowners were also required to keep a watercourse within its banks, deal with flood damage and keep a stream clear of blockages. The imprecision invited legal challenges to test or avoid responsibilities and until new powers were created property owners continued to determine how rivers were maintained.

Major infrastructure incidents were dealt with by specially appointed one-off commissions— like the commissions *de Wallis et Fossatis* dealing with flooding from the Thames breaches. It was not until the sixteenth century that this principle of a supra-judicial commission was extended to cover the day-to-day business of maintaining rivers when the 1531 Statute of Sewers led to the creation of London Sewers Commissions, primarily *pro conservacione murorum mariscorum* (for the maintaining of the sea walls), but also with responsibility for the rivers and stream. Separate commissions took responsibility for the different areas: the City, Tower Hamlets and Holborn, while South London and the Effra was under the jurisdiction of the Surrey and Kent Commissioners. Their territory notionally extended from the River Mole at Molesey to the River Ravensbourne at Deptford but their main preoccupation was with the low-lying and densely populated stretch of land between Battersea and Deptford and its problems of drainage and flooding.

In 1554 when the Surrey and Kent Commission was set up, the 'sewers' of their title did not encompass the word's modern meaning of the removal of sewage. Their role covered land drainage and the prevention of flooding by surveying, repairing, 'clensing' and 'scowring' river walls and water courses and then identifying and charging the landowners for their work. It is from their scrupulously kept minutes that we extract some of the earliest detail about the Effra.

The Commissioners did constant battle on two fronts: with nature and with recalcitrant landowners. A typical entry relating to the Clapham Road sewer in 1573 requires the landowner to 'grave and pluck out the wedes out of the sewer as to cut up the bushes and willows growing on eyther side'. Another entry from December that same year instructs William Esinn and Thomas Etherige at Kennington, to 'clense & skore' the sewer between their lands, making it eighteen inches deeper and at least eight feet wide at the narrowest part; Esinn was also required to 'make and set uppe a substancialle grate of Oken timber' at the point it entered the main stream of the Effra at Kennington Common (so that the flow from his sewer would not blow-back and flood the fields). They were given four months after which they would be fined twenty pence for each rod of sewer not done, and ten pence if the oak grate had not been 'sett hanginge'.[11]

By the eighteenth century, as the number of houses along the Effra in Vauxhall, South Lambeth and Kennington and the incidences of blockages and flooding increased, the cumbersome system of charging individual landholders was replaced by a general sewers rate to fund the costs of the works. What had started off as an ad hoc judicial commission was turning into an established piece of local government. The Commissioners still tended to be a subset of the local landowning great and good who found it helpful to sit on the Commission. Just occasionally there is a sense of a sort of local democracy at work, as when in 1780 the 'inhabitants of Kennington' raise a complaint against Joseph Mawbey, himself a Commissioner, that the common sewer running through to his lands to Vauxhall Creek be 'cast and clensed'.

Much of the work was small-scale, petty even: a never-ending pursuit of the constructors of rogue bridges (like the one serving the Lawn on South Lambeth Road discovered in 1821) or the installers of unauthorised sluice gates. In 1825 a rogue sewer was found to have been dug from the newly-built houses of South Island Place to the Effra by being cut through the stone arch of the bridge at Clapham Road. Often the perpetrators were merely required to appear before the Commission to be 'admonished'; only occasionally was a fine levied or action enforced.

In its initial incarnation the Commission's responsibility had been to ensure that the Effra, along with its networks of smaller sewers, ditches and field drains, functioned effectively as river and surface water drainage for low-lying Lambeth and that everything, literally, flowed smoothly. But from the beginning of the nineteenth century a new type of drainage was becoming more of a concern as the sewers that the Commissioners were responsible for began to take on the modern sense of 'channels for carrying off sewage'. The Effra and its tributary ditches were increasingly serving as conduits for house drainage and house waste. In 1828 the Commissioners met to agree on the wording of a notice 'cautioning the public against throwing

---

11   London County Council, *Court Minutes of the Surrey and Kent Sewers Commission*, vol. 1, 1909, p. 135 and pp. 177-8

nightsoil or rubbish into sewers drains or watercourses'. It was not that they were opposed to the Effra being used for sewage disposal, rather that if it were to be done, it should be done on their terms. These nightsoil collectors were objected to because they had not sought permission and paid for the privilege, not because of any concern about pollution or public health.

The Commissioners' approach to waste disposal combined *ad hoc* permissions for individual householders and negotiated agreements for larger pieces of drainage works. In 1821 John Mullins paid £2 10 shillings 'to make a drain into the Washway [the local name for the Effra] at North Brixton in front of his two houses'. In 1825 Lord Holland's agent approached the Commissioners seeking to develop his estate between Coldharbour Lane and Loughborough House into new streets (Barrington Road and Sussex Road) and to construct a new drain from these villas to join the Effra on Brixton Road.[12] The printed particulars advertising the venture addressed to would-be builders stressed that 'the whole land will admit of excellent drainage at a moderate expense'.[13] There was a further approach from the estate in 1843 by its architect, Henry Currey, who paid the Commission £1,224 towards the cost of draining the new houses 'on the north side of Coldharbour Lane, North Brixton' into the Effra sewer.[14]

By the 1840s, South Lambeth Road and Kennington Oval were already developed for housing and the Commissioners had realised that the Effra was actually a development asset that could be monetised by providing an easy drainage route for new houses now needing to be built with modern plumbing. This had the effect of transforming the Effra valley between Kennington and Brixton into something of a development corridor whose landowners were hastening to cash in their market gardens and redeem them as housing. 'The proprietors of all the lands of North Brixton and its neighbourhood east and west, have been enabled to convert them into building ground of a very profitable description, and to realise rents which half a century since could never have been anticipated.'[15]

The increasing fashion for the new flushing toilets was to have a dramatic effect on the river. The adoption of the water closet by London's middle classes dated from the beginning of the nineteenth century when the earlier 'pan' and 'valve' closets were superseded by more sophisticated models like the 'hopper'. By 1822 a standard builders' manual could declare that there 'is no good house without one' and by the middle of the century some more status-conscious households even had their drainage plans on display engraved on a brass plaque.[16] To install a water closet required two givens: a supply of piped water in and a drainage route out into a sewer. Many thousands of new houses were being built around the edges of London and the volume of waste water created was far beyond the capacity of a few cess pools dug out by nightsoil men. The timings of the two key elements were awry; the piped water was now on hand, brought from the Lambeth Water Company's reservoir on Brixton Hill, but the sewers were not yet built. This gap between the enthusiastic adoption of the flushing toilet and the

---

12 Sewers Commission minutes, SKCS/59/420, (LMA)
13 Sewers Commission plans, SKCS/P3/87, (LMA)
14 Sewers Commission minutes, SKCS/65 & SKCS/67, (LMA)
15 *Reports Relating to the Sewage*, SKCS, 1843 (LMA)
16 *The English Terraced House*, Stefan Muthesius, 1982

creation of its supporting drainage system was a major problem across London and would rapidly transform the Effra from a small river into a big sewer (See Plate 7).

The Commissioners were engaged in a difficult balancing act. As the suburbs of London expanded south so yet more house building upstream created more pollution downstream. As they approved drainage schemes for new developments upriver, so the Commissioners were being confronted by angry householders living downstream. The residents of South Lambeth Road were writing to their MP; house owners on Kennington Oval were withholding their sewer rates because of the filthy stream; and the residents of Brixton Road were campaigning for the Effra flowing past their front gardens to be covered over. This latter protest against 'the effluvia arising therefrom which was dangerous to the health of the inhabitants' had begun in 1834 and was to drag on for thirteen years with repeated petitions and memorials from the well-connected residents.

The year 1847 was the final one of Sewer Commissioners' jurisdiction. Even as they were contesting the passage through Parliament of the bill that would abolish them, the Commissioners were still fighting on all fronts. Perhaps rather belatedly, they had approached the scientist Sir Michael Faraday to seek his help in developing some chemical solution for 'removing or destroying noxious vapours' from their sewers (he declined to help). At the same time they were denying responsibility for the claims by Mr Aylwin of Loughborough Road that his children's illness was caused by their open sewer, as well as discouraging a housing development around Coldharbour Lane and Denmark Hill that would drain into the Effra, arguing that 'funds were not available for that vicinity'. The much-delayed covering over of the remaining open stretch of the Effra along Brixton Road was about to happen; the residents had come up with £7,500 towards its cost and the Angell Estate (now on the point of laying out the streets of its new suburb, Angell Town) was also prepared to contribute to the cost. Then finally in November, in the very last month of their existence, the Commissioners were approached by another developer seeking to build a suburb of houses even further upriver in Dulwich, the drainage of which would also 'be effected by the upper part of the Effra'.[17]

The suburban process in Lambeth and across London was becoming unstoppable as landowners switched from agriculture to the more lucrative returns from laying out streets of houses. For the moment there was only one destination for the inevitable human by-products of that land speculation in Lambeth—they ended up in the River Effra. The Commissioners, stuck with playing to an old set of rules that gave them neither the funding nor the powers to deal with this rapidly changing landscape, sat and waited for their services to be dispensed with.

---

17   Sewer Commission minutes, 1847, SKCS/68, (LMA)

3

IN THE STABLES OF AUGEAS

A large and detailed plan held in the Lambeth Archives[1] gives a snapshot of the development of the Holland and Angell estates in the Effra valley at North Brixton in 1850. It shows a network of newly-built streets, set among the last of the turnip fields and nursery grounds and bisected by open drains and ditches which drain eastwards into the Effra just off the edge of the map. The lines of Barrington Road, Sussex Road, Millbrook Row, Coldharbour Lane and Loughborough Park are edged with unsold building plots, terraces of new housing and larger detached villas, many still under construction ('Building in January 1850'). The finished houses have their aspirational builders' names: Russell Terrace, Pelican House, Belgrave Terrace. This plan is much more than just a glimpse of suburbia in the making. Its purpose was to record the provision of drainage and this townscape of new roads and drains and old ditches has been peppered with tiny neatly-inked observations: '4 feet of water and deposit', 'materials and workmanship bad', 'covered with wood', '6 inches of solid deposit' and, most of all, the regularly repeated comment, 'no smell'. The euphemistic 'deposits' and the negative information about smell suggest an obvious conclusion: mostly it stank.

But what this plan really reveals —just one year after cholera had killed 14,000 people across London and over 2,000 in Lambeth—is the ramshackle precariousness of the suburban free-for-all that was taking place around the edges of London as thousands of new houses without any proper drainage were being thrown up. In its quiet way it is as emblematic of the contradictions of Victorian modernity as Dickens' description of the railway being built through Camden Town in *Dombey and Son* or Turner's painting *The Fighting Temeraire*. This zone of half-built cheap stuccoed structures with their stick-on Italianate porches set between scraps of muddy field and threaded with open ditches in which human faeces slowly flow towards the River Effra was a public health disaster waiting to happen. Yet instead of being depicted by a novelist, a campaigning journalist or an artist, it is the work of a forgotten surveyor with a nose for detail.

That 'solid deposit' pooling in the ditches of North Brixton eventually slid its way off the map down the open ditch running along the side of Loughborough Road and dropped into the arched-over Effra by the White Horse pub (now the Brixton Jamm). It would have bobbed its way north in the dark along the length of Brixton Road, skirted the churchyard of St Mark's Church at Kennington (arched over in 1838 so that those confronting human mortality might not simultaneously confront human feculence), passed under Clapham Road before

---

1   North Brixton Sewers, 1850, LBL/DES/DRG/1/1 (LAD)

re-emerging into the sunshine—to the extreme, but impotent, annoyance of the householders of Hanover Place—to process slowly around the outer edge of The Oval before turning into South Lambeth Road to pause outside the house of Mr John Thomas.

In June 1850, the same year that the plan was surveyed, Mr Thomas was in a foul mood; when he picked up pen to write to *The Times* his language was more direct than that used by the surveyor. 'Three feet of excrement always exposed to the lungs of the neighbouring population,' he raged. 'Were the cholera here now, it would revel in this Lethe of filth and abomination.' From John Thomas' house the 'solid deposit' was then carried through the panting darkness beneath the recently opened railway line at Vauxhall Station and under the Wandsworth Road beneath Cox's Bridge. Coming back into the sunlight of Vauxhall Creek, it paused once more among the barges of Price's candle works as it waited for the tide to turn, then, bumping against the wooden campshedding at the mouth of the Effra, it bravely entered the Thames just upstream of Vauxhall Bridge.

In 1848 the Metropolitan Commission of Sewers, the body which would create that plan of North Brixton, had taken over the functions of the seven former London Sewers Commissions. Edwin Chadwick's 1842 *Sanitary Report* had lambasted the old Commissioners as 'uncertain, erroneous and defective in their general principles of construction, injurious in their actions and unduly expensive'. It may have been simplistic and overstated, but it struck a common chord: 'The Commissioners of Sewers ought to be well rolled in their filthy ditches before going to any of their splendid London Tavern dinners' was one typical response.[2] More usefully, Chadwick's report provided the political justification for replacing the seven bickering, byzantine and rather complacent institutions with a single body to deal more effectively with London's drainage.

Constituted by the 1848 Metropolitan Sewers Act, the Metropolitan Commission was given powers over all London's rivers and watercourse extending 'twelve miles distant from St Paul's'. Public health, rather than land drainage, was now the main driver. The Commissioners had the powers to 'abate' watercourses that were 'prejudicial to the health of the neighbourhood' and new houses had to be built connected to existing public sewers, which of course rather raised the question: what public sewers? The provision of a main drainage system for London became the Commission's principal objective. As an organisation it was defined in part by the selection of its Commissioners; the inclusion of civil engineers and railway builders like Robert Stephenson and William Cubitt as well as key figures from the Ordnance Survey suggested a new and refreshing scientific and practical rigour.

---

2   *Report of the Health of London Association on the Sanitary Condition of the Metropolis*, section 10, 1847

A necessary precursor to any London drainage scheme was the mapping of its existing watercourses and sewers. Worryingly, many of the old Sewers Commissioners did not actually know the location or routes of many of these. Before 1847 the Surrey and Kent Commissioners had only really concerned themselves with the lower reaches of the Effra where flooding and drainage impacted on property. The river above Brixton, out in the bad-lands of Dulwich and Norwood, was a *terra incognita* of straw-sucking rural idiocy as far as the Commissioners, urbanely installed in their office in Newington court house, were concerned. Flowing through a barely populated agricultural landscape it had been a matter of indifference to them whether the upper Effra was blocked or flooded. No one complained and it could be ignored.

So one of the Commissioners' first acts was to initiate a survey of all the sewers and watercourses in the Metropolitan area. For the next four years, its surveyors fanned out around London, armed with red leather notebooks in which they made detailed pencil sketches and recorded meticulously the distance, level variation and altitude above datum of every sewer. The contour watershed lines of the basins of the Effra, Wandle, Ravensbourne were walked, mapped

Investigation of the River Effra at Norwood Common, now Norwood Park, ca. 1860.

and levelled. Such precise information had never been assembled before. It was precious, and to reduce the risk of loss each of the 1,365 surviving surveyors' notebooks has inked on its title page the promise of a two shillings and sixpence reward for anyone finding the book and returning it to the Commission's offices.[3] The original intention had been for the Metropolitan Commission to work with the Ordnance Survey to produce a complete large-scale published map series of London showing sewers and house drainage. This was not immediately realised and many local series of plans—like the one for North Brixton—were drawn up instead.

In 1849 the Commissioners had invited proposals from the public for schemes for London's drainage. They received over 130 submissions and it fell to Joseph Bazalgette, a thirty-year-old engineer with previous experience of working on railways and land drainage and just appointed assistant surveyor to the Commission, to help adjudicate on the merits of the different schemes. The Commission's preferred model duly emerged: two networks of 'combined' (surface water and sewage) intercepting sewers to the north and south sides of London would carry the waste out east to the Thames estuary, so keeping the river 'within the Metropolitan districts free from sewage at all times of the tide'.[4] The detail still had to be developed, but the basic shape of the scheme was in place by 1850.

The main difficulty was how to finance it. The Commission's annual budget of £200,000 came from the sewer rates; these were exacted locally and were already a hugely resented central imposition. Lambeth Vestry's petition of complaint to the Commission in 1850 was typical, arguing for local boards with 'local knowledge and business habits' rather than an 'inefficient and injurious' centralised Commission whose rates were now double those of the old Surrey and Kent Commissioners.[5] Double or not, and while the Commission could still make progress with surveying, the real issue was that it had not been given the political or financial powers to obtain the enormous funding required for a major project that would cost over £2,000,000.

In 1855 the Metropolis Management Act replaced the Metropolitan Commission of Sewers with a new democratically elected London body, the Metropolitan Board of Works, with the means to raise such sums. It signalled central government's recognition that such a major piece of infrastructure would have to be a properly funded and empowered public work. There was much opposition from 'anti-centralists' preoccupied with property rights as well as from private water companies, local paving boards and parish vestries. These were some of the vested interests opposed to a notion of 'public health' which were ridiculed by John Snow for espousing 'that form of liberty to which some communities still cling, the sacred power to poison to death not only themselves but their neighbours'.[6] In 1852 Joseph Bazalgette had been promoted to chief engineer of the Commission and now in 1855 he moved across to hold the same post for the Board of Works; a year later he would present his fully worked-up scheme for London's main drainage.

---

3   MCS/498 series, 1848-52 (LMA)
4   *Report on the Drainage of the north districts of the River Thames*, 1851, MCS/478/004 (LMA)
5   Lambeth Vestry minutes, P3/7, pp. 199-203 (LAD)
6   Dr John Snow, speaking at the Bristol Social Science Congress, 1849

Under Bazalgette's scheme the River Effra would disappear underground into a sewer for its entire length and its stream above Brixton would flow into intercepting sewers, to help drive the household waste of south-east London out to the Southern Outfall at Crossness. However, as it was still uncertain not just when and how, but even at times whether, the scheme would actually be funded and realised, so the Board was also obliged to continue with the piecemeal covering over of the Effra that had begun in the 1820s.

In such a parsimonious climate only those works where third parties contributed to the costs, or where the Board was subjected to sustained political lobbying, tended to happen. So the open stream alongside the recently built police station on Canterbury Road (now Crescent) in Brixton was covered over in 1857 after the Metropolitan Police Commission agreed to pay for it.[7] It took eleven years of memorials and petitions to Lambeth Vestry and the Board (and some deaths from 'low fever') for the householders of Hanover Place (now Gardens) at Kennington Oval to have their length of badly polluted river covered over in 1860. Then, in 1862, two large contracts were issued for the diversion into a sewer of a mile-and-a-half stretch of the Effra from Brixton police station along Dulwich Road south to Herne Hill railway station.[8] Again, this happened because the contracts coincided with the construction by the London Chatham and Dover Railway of the line between Brixton and Herne Hill, with the company willing to meet 25 per cent of the £4,000 cost, and because of determined lobbying by the residents on Dulwich Road.[9] The Brixton contract (also lobbied for by Lambeth Vestry, wishing to divert the Effra on to public roads and away from private land) angled tidily along Brixton Water Lane and Effra Road to drain and so freed up for development future sites in central Brixton such as for example the covered markets. The same approach was taken in diverting the Effra around Norwood Cemetery onto Norwood High Street ('abandoning as far as practical the course of the open Effra which runs mostly through private property and is difficult of access'[10]), which must have delighted the cemetery company's shareholders given that a polluted stream flooding their grave plots was not conducive to business.

But all of these local works were but remedial footnotes to Bazalgette's *grand projet*. There were other householder and business applicants along the Effra who could not contribute to the cost or who lacked sufficient influence, like Mr Porter at Coldharbour Lane who was stonewalled with the Board's standard response ('the construction of the main drainage is the only permanent remedy for the evil of which he complains'): until it had made up its mind what form that construction would take the Board was not going to spend any more money on partial solutions.[11]

Almost ten years later, just how that 'permanent remedy' was to be achieved remained unclear. In 1858 the scheme was in danger of stalling because of its increasing cost, now projected at over £3,000,000, and because of political bickering between the Board and the (unelected) Royal Commission of Works and Public Buildings, which had been given power of veto over the scheme. It would take the hot summer of 1858, known as the 'Great Stink', to break that deadlock.

---

7   MBW minutes, June 1856
8   MBW Contracts, MBW/2426/30 and 33, 1862 (LMA)
9   Lambeth Sewers Committee, 1862, P3/139/1, (LAD); MBW minutes
10 Lambeth Vestry minutes, 1862, P3/12 (LAD)
11 MBW minutes, October 1856

The unusually poisonous stench from the untreated sewage in the Thames outside the Houses of Parliament that summer so overpowered MPs—which must have seemed poisonously ironic given the subject under debate—that it served to stampede the situation; enabling legislation was quickly passed preventing legal and parliamentary challenges to the scheme, removing the Royal Commission's veto and permitting the Board to raise bonds underwritten by the Treasury against future ratable income over the next forty years in order to fund the main drainage scheme.

Over the next eight years the Northern and Southern intercepting sewer systems —London's largest ever infrastructure project — were slowly tunnelled and constructed out to their Thames outfalls at Barking and Crossness. Demand for materials and labour for the building works created a local inflationary spike: the price of bricks increased by 40 to 50 per cent and skilled workmen's wages by 20 per cent and many other building projects in London simply went on hold. Where possible the new intercepting sewers followed existing road lines: it was easier to obtain access during construction and afterwards for maintenance, as was dealing with a single local authority rather than having to treat with multiple landowners. So the Southern High Level, passing from Clapham through Stockwell to cross the Effra at Brixton, followed the lines of Landor Road, Sidney Street and Robsart Street to Brixton Road. Continuing east along Loughborough Road it

The Southern High Level Sewer under construction at Peckham, 1862.

had to cross the still undeveloped market gardens of the Minet Estate where it incurred additional expenses as both the owner, William Minet, and one of his tenants, William Myatt, lodged claims for damage to land and crops from the excavations.[12]

Progress was covered approvingly in the press and celebratory official openings at the northern and southern outfalls took place in 1865 and 1868. Perhaps to keep them sweet, the Board had also invited London's vestrymen along to a jolly to inspect the then near-complete works in 1864. Frederick Doulton, who combined the ownership of a local pottery works with serving as both a Lambeth vestryman and as the Lambeth member on the Board of Works, laid on a private steamer for his colleagues. Noting that they had not all dined together since 1856, Lambeth Vestry then 'determined on the present occasion to cater liberally for the comfort and enjoyment of their colleagues' and laid on a dinner at Greenwich after the visit which was enjoyed 'with apparent great satisfaction'.[13] A slightly different account of the same event in one London newspaper suggests 'a most indecorous scene marred what had hitherto been a merry gathering' when inebriated vestrymen pelted one of the presumably rather bumptious members for St Pancras with bread rolls, engaged in barefoot races along the beach of the Thames and, in some instances, were so incapacitated that they could not find their return steamer and had to be helped onto a train.[14]

Drunken vestrymen aside, there was no denying the achievement of the Metropolitan Board of Works and its chief engineer in creating a main drainage system for London. It was a benefit on so many levels: a triumph of civil engineering; an object lesson in the provision of 'Public Health'; and a victory for public good over individual property rights and greedy self-interest. The Effra, depending on the individual's perspective, was either improved or lost. Bazalgette the *prestidigitateur* had made that particular white rabbit vanish into his black hat.

Two things had happened to the Effra. The first was that the piecemeal covering-over that had begun in the 1820s was replaced by a complete culverting of the river into brick sewers. The second was that the underground river's natural flow was interrupted by three new intercepting sewers, running west to east along the contours, which now carried all South London's sewage and surface water to the Southern Outfall at Crossness. From north to south these three sewers were: the Southern Low Level, which started in Putney, crossed the Effra by Vauxhall Station, flowed parallel with it but in the opposite direction around Kennington Oval and then flowed east through Camberwell; the Southern High Level, which began in Clapham, flowed through Stockwell, crossed the Effra at the junction of Brixton Road and Loughborough Road and then passed on through Peckham; and finally the Effra Branch, which began at the point where the two main branches of the Effra (the Upper Norwood and the Lower Norwood) met at Croxted Road, ducked around the contour lines of Belair Park to run north-east beneath Dulwich and Nunhead to join the High Level at New Cross. The High and Low Levels then combined at Deptford, crossed the creek of the Ravensbourne and flowed east across Plumstead Marshes to enter the Thames at Crossness.

---

12   MBW minutes, April 1860
13   Lambeth Vestry minutes, July 1864, P3/ (LAD)
14   *Marylebone Mercury*, 30 July 1864

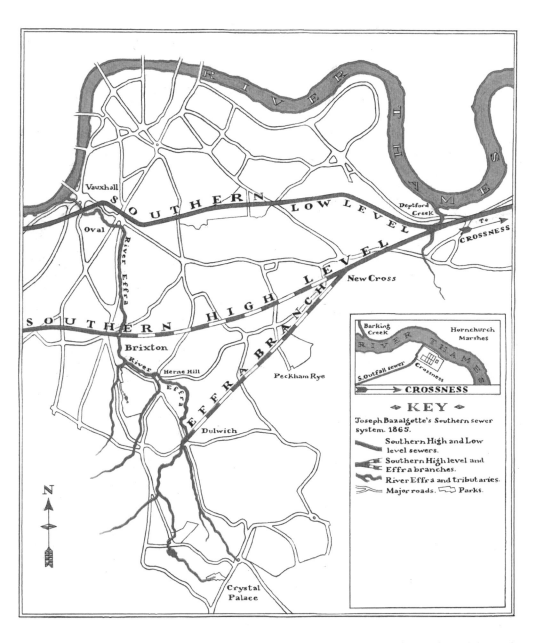

A plan showing how the Bazalgette's intercepting sewers abstracted the flow of the Effra and diverted it to the Southern Outfall at Crossness after 1865.

Crucially these intercepting sewers now drained away most of the waters of the Effra. The Upper and Lower Norwood branches vanished into the ten-foot brick invert of the Effra Branch sewer, while the waters from those lower tributaries at Brockwell Park, Norwood Road and Dulwich joining the Effra downstream were siphoned off by the Southern High Level at Brixton Road. The course of the Effra beyond Brixton was virtually dry.

Although the lower river had doubly disappeared, its course gone underground into sewers and with its flow siphoned east to Crossness, the Effra's bed still remained visible in just a few places. The northern section above Herne Hill, the Upper Norwood branch and the southern half of the Lower Norwood branch were all out of sight. The instructions on the contract drawings had been quite explicit: 'Ditch to be filled in. Existing sewer to be broken up.' By 1870 the only remaining visible stretch of the Effra was that section of the Lower Norwood branch running from the north of Norwood Cemetery across Rosendale Road, Croxted Road through Dulwich to Herne Hill.

Over the next five years the remains of the dry channel north of the cemetery was filled in and laid out as a tight grid of terraced streets; the loop through Dulwich underwent the

The remains of the Effra's water meadows at Norwood, between Lancaster Avenue and Rosendale Road. When the photograph was taken in ca 1870 the course of the river was already dry.

same treatment in the 1890s when Burbage Road and Turney Road were laid out. This was under the aegis of the paternalistic Dulwich Estate rather than via the free-for-all development seen in Norwood, so these houses were larger and surrounded by a green leaven of cricket pitches, tennis courts and sports fields. But the end result was the same; by 1895 the Effra had disappeared from the surface of South London.

Like the residents of Brixton Road and Hanover Place, who had campaigned for its dirty, rubbish-clogged stream to be covered over, most people living close to the river appreciated what had been done. But not everyone celebrated: Mr Alderson, a market gardener at Langley Lane, South Lambeth, complaining of his loss of irrigation, argued that the Board should provide him with a fresh water supply as the Effra had been 'a natural stream'. The residents of The Lawn, a Georgian terrace on South Lambeth Road, sought compensation for the loss of the ornamental water in front of their homes which was now drained away, while several landowners along the Upper Norwood branch whose boundaries had been defined by the Effra tried to claim the cost of replacement boundary fencing.[15] All these claims, based on riparian rights under Common Law, were rejected.

But if the Board's legal arguments were generally watertight, the same could not be said of its main drainage system after heavy rainfall. The Effra, despite being bundled away out of sight, continued to flood. Clearly all rivers flood from time to time, even one as disarmingly small as the Effra, and it had done so regularly. In May 1818, for example, after 'heavy and incessant rain' Brixton Washway (Brixton Road) 'had the appearance of a large lake'. Local businesses flooded out included a brewer, a brickmaker and a market gardener, and at least two local people drowned: the severely bruised body of the landlord of the White Horse at Brixton, who was washed downstream, was found trapped in a flood gate by Kennington Oval.[16]

Small-scale disasters drained away and tended to get forgotten, but as the fields on each side of the Effra were built over, so the flood damage became more pronounced. In November 1839, again after days of heavy rainfall, an 'immense body of land water flowing down the Effra towards the river' met the tide coming upstream from the Thames along Brixton Road and 'caused all that part to be inundated, the lower floors of the houses having five foot of water in them and the streets being nearly impassable'.[17] Again in 1860, after Brixton Road had endured another 'calamitous inundation', the residents petitioned the Metropolitan Board of Works, suggesting that blockages downstream must have caused the flooding. The Board duly investigated, found itself not liable, blamed the heavy rainfall and in what was now their default response to any complaints, declared that the solution was the system of intercepting main drainage that they were in the process of constructing.[18]

The Board believed that once the Effra had ceased to be a river and was contained within sewers then the problem of flooding would be solved as the wide bore of the intercepting sewers would cope with such surges in surface water after heavy rainfall. Then in April 1878, after twelve hours of 'a continuous heavy downpour of rain which at times fell with almost tropical violence', and coinciding with a high tide in the Thames driving south down Vauxhall Creek, the Effra

15 MBW minutes, 1864 and 1866
16 *The Times*, 12-17 May 1818
17 *The Times*, 30 November 1839
18 MBW minutes, September 1860

frighteningly re-emerged. 'Yesterday morning at half past seven it was seen to issue out of the sewer in Brixton Road and in a short time nearly the whole length of the road from the Brixton Railway Station to Kennington Common was covered by a rushing stream of water extending from pathway to pathway and in some places from house to house.' Vassall Road became a raging channel of water feeding into Camberwell New Road, which was also flooded.[19]

There had been a similarly devastating flood of the Falcon Brook in Battersea in the previous August and the Board, realising that the system was unable to cope with exceptional rain, had a rather Heath Robinson solution ready to run immediately after the Brixton flood. Six obsolete railway locomotives, which the Board had purchased from the Great Western Railway, were converted into stationary pumping engines: one at the mouth of the Effra, others at the Falcon Brook and Crossness. The Effra pumping engine at Vauxhall Cross was mounted on an arch over Vauxhall Creek and powered a centrifuge pump in a chamber adjacent to the sewer; after heavy rainfall or tidal surge it would pump water into the Thames to stop it surging back up the Effra to flood Brixton and Kennington.

In its 1879 annual report the Board admitted that the Southern High and Low Level sewers were incapable of dealing with extreme rainfall: to do so 'would have necessitated intercepting channels of the capacity of rivers', which would have been unaffordable.[20] Bazalgette's original drainage scheme was over twenty years old and 'the whole circumstances of the Metropolis had undergone a complete and an extraordinary change that could never have been anticipated.'[21] The scheme had been drawn up when London had 300,000 houses and now there were 500,000 whose additional drainage was threatening to overwhelm the system. Having once set up London's drainage, the Board of Works and its successors would for ever be obliged to extend it to keep pace with urban growth.

Converted railway locomotives were clearly only a temporary solution. In 1879 the Lambeth surveyor noted that 600 of the 1,400 houses in the neighbourhood of the White Horse at Brixton were liable to flooding, and that the Board of Works was about to convert the Effra Sewer between Brixton and Vauxhall Creek into a storm overflow to relieve the pressure on the Southern High Level. Lambeth would have to construct a replacement sewer for ordinary household drainage. This shifting of responsibility by the Board provoked much local muttering : the High Level Sewer 'conferred an advantage upon distant localities [but] brought baneful consequences upon Brixton and Stockwell'.[22] Nevertheless, by 1890 this new network of storm relief sewers was in place, the temporary pumping engine at Vauxhall Creek was replaced and the creek itself, for over 600 years the mouth of the river, was sealed off as a self-contained dock. The storm water flows were directed instead to two new outfalls (serving the combined Heathwall, Duffield and Effra storm relief sewers) built beneath Vauxhall Bridge. They are still there and are wrongly believed by many people to be the mouth of the river—which is something of a paradox given that they actually represent that moment when the lower Effra ceased to be a 'river' in any accepted sense of that word and turned into an emergency storm drain.

The storm relief sewers mostly did their job, and there were no more damaging inundations

19   *The Times*, 12 April 1878
20   *Annual Report of the Metropolitan Board of Works*, 1878-9 (LMA)
21   *The Builder*, 9 August 1879
22   Lambeth Vestry minutes P3/21/ p. 382; P3/22/ p. 82, 1879 -80 (LAD)

Flooding caused by the Effra at Wood Street, now Dunelm Grove, Norwood, 1914.

in Kennington or North Brixton, but the upper Effra above the Southern High Level still functioned to an extent as a river. During heavy rainfall its flow when combined with drainage and surface water could still cause spectacular flooding. So, in June 1914, after three hours of torrential rain and thunderstorms, dozens of streets in Norwood either side of the cemetery were swamped. 'The ground floors of the houses were all flooded and in some cases Sunday joints were washed out of ovens.' Dozens of the temporarily homeless spent the night on the floor of the public hall on Knights Hill (now the Portico Gallery) and a parish relief fund was set up to help the victims. The flooding problems in Norwood recurred until this section of the Effra sewer was enlarged in 1935.[23]

As London grew through the twentieth century, so its drainage system continued to be expanded to meet the need for additional exit routes for sewage and surface water and the course of the Effra became just one of now multiple drainage routes. Multiplicity does not absolutely guarantee security and ongoing occasional inundations, of which the flood at Herne Hill and Dulwich in 2004 was the most recent, are reminders that in its upper reaches at least, the Effra is still there and can return to surprise us.

---

23   *The Story of Norwood*, J.B. Wilson, 1973

4

WHAT'S IN A NAME?

'The Effra, doubtless shortened from Effrena, meaning unbridled river'
John Ruskin, *Praeterita*, 1884

In South London around Brixton, Herne Hill, Norwood and Dulwich the word Effra is almost a commonplace; it provides the name for two roads (and is alluded to in others), a pub, a bar and a café, several blocks of flats, a business centre, a day care centre, a children's centre, a local band, a locally brewed beer and a football club—not to mention a secure mental health ward in a nearby hospital and a friend's black Labrador. It is a word that is embedded in the local linguistic landscape while at the same time, rather like the course of the hidden river it represents, it contains a surprising amount of uncertainty, disagreement even, about where the name comes from and what it means.

Perhaps unusually for a man who took pride in his scholarship and precise use of language, Ruskin gets his definition, 'doubtless shortened from Effrena', horribly wrong. English river names are either pre-Roman or else derive from later Saxon or Viking words, but they are never Roman or Latinate. In 1864 Isaac Taylor, an influential figure in English place-name research, declared, 'There are very few river names that are not Celtic',[1] and Victorian philologists set about establishing Celtic or Brittonic derivations for local river names. The Thames itself and some of its larger tributaries (Brent, Lea, Darent) are now known to be Celtic in origin. Unsurprisingly, local writers sought to uncover a Celtic etymology for the name Effra as well. Writing just fifteen years after Ruskin, the London historian Walter Besant appears to be the first to suggest the Celtic *Yfrid*, meaning torrent, as the probable root word.[2] It might have been appropriate for the stretch of stream coming down the Norwood hills in mid-winter but perhaps a misnomer for most of its subsequent sluggish course; it was, of course, an imaginative leap for Besant writing in 1899 when the river could no longer be seen. His attribution stuck and has been re-cited by many subsequent and reputable sources so as to pass into general acceptance.[3]

Behind the survival of Celtic river names is an assumption about the primacy of established name use. The earlier Celtic or Brythonic names for landscape features like hills and rivers, which often had local religious associations, were retained by later Roman, Saxon, Viking and Norman invader/settlers, whereas they would create new namings in their own

---

1   *Words and Places*, Isaac Taylor, 1864
2   *London South of the Thames*, Sir Walter Besant, 1899
3   *The Lost Rivers of London*, Nicholas Barton, 1962; *The London Encyclopaedia*, Christopher Hibbert, ed., 1983; *Thames: Sacred River*, Peter Ackroyd, 2007—and many more.

language for their own farms and settlements. Yet this does not mean that all, particularly smaller, river names are Celtic in origin. Many of the Thames' other London tributaries are Anglo-Saxon (the Peck, the Tyburn, the Fleet and the Walbrook), while others, like the Mole and the Wandle, are Anglo-Saxon 'back-formations' from the place-names of the settlements they pass through.

In other words, a recovered Celtic etymology does not always work, and there have been at least two other suggested derivations for Effra from different linguistic routes. The Anglo-Saxon contender, noting the landmark Heah Yfre or Hegefre, found in two Saxon charters describing the boundaries of Battersea,[4] goes on to suggest that this referred to the mouth of the Effra. 'Efre is perhaps the higher ground between that stream and the watercourse which runs out just west of it.'[5] Apart from now knowing, with the benefit of hindsight, that the pre-medieval Effra did not enter the Thames at Vauxhall, never mind yet carry that name, the boundary feature in question cannot be the River Effra which never, even in its later diversion, marked the boundary with Battersea parish. The Heah Efre referred to in these charters has to be the nearby Heathwall Sluice, which did provide that boundary. Yfre/Efre is a variant of the more common *ofer*, 'bank, river bank, shore', and Hegefre has been translated as 'high bank'. Heathwall (previously Hesewall, Hethewall) also refers to an embankment of some kind beside which the later Heathwall Sluice entered the Thames. So while Heathwall and Heah Yfre are probably not actual variants of the same name, they are likely to be different names for the same topographical feature—the late Saxon river wall that protected Battersea and Lambeth from flooding—and nothing to do with the River Effra.

If Celtic was the go-to language of the nineteenth-century place-name historian, then Proto-Germanic, that artificial and retrospective recreation of a Germanic root language by late twentieth-century linguistic historians, is the language of choice for some more recent essays in place-naming. So, the Proto-Germanic *ēþrō, via the Old English *ǣðre*—'runlet of water, fountain, spring, stream'—is the latest dubious suggested derivation.[6]

The major difficulty for any of these alternative etymologies is the fact that there have been no historical variants to the name Effra. Most other London river names have been documented from the medieval period or even back to Anglo-Saxon charters, and it is the earlier variant spellings of their names that allow conclusions to be drawn about their derivation. The Effra, not found as a river name until the early nineteenth century, is a startlingly recent adoption that has undergone no changes, making any of the suggested derivations little more than educated guesswork.

---

4   *The Early Charters of Eastern England*, C.R. Hart, 1966; *Anglo Saxon Charters*, P.H. Sawyer, 1968

5   *Place Names of Surrey*, English Place Names Society, vol. XI, 1969, also acknowledging that 'Except as an antiquarian revival, OE *efre* could not appear as Modern English *Effra*.'

6   Wikipedia, referenced March 2016. It has been pointed out that 'this assumes a dental fricative /ð/ turn into a labiodental fricative /f/? If that is an attested sound-change (and they are generally reliable in their consistency), then why didn't (for example) the Saxon king's name Æðelred become Effelred in later times?' Personal communication with Gareth King.

In the fourteenth-century court records the 'new cut' between Kennington and Vauxhall is simply referred to as a *fossatum*, a ditch or dyke, while older sections of the stream get the equally generic 'waterweye' or 'comennflodytch'. By the mid-sixteenth century, the Commissioners of Sewers were using recognisable names for most of South London's rivers: the Earl's Sluice, the Ravensbourne at Deptford, the Neckinger ('Devells Neckercher') and the Wandle (simply 'the river') are all recorded in their minutes. But the Effra remains the anonymous, or polyonymous, exception, going under a variety of local names or aliases. In South Lambeth and Vauxhall it was the 'South Lambeth ditch', the 'Winterbourne sewer', the 'Main sewer' or the 'Common sewer'; in the eighteenth century the Manor of Kennington called it the 'New River'. The section of the stream flowing south of Kennington Common along Brixton Road was referred to as the Washway (from the Old English *Waesse*, a swamp with the derived sense of a stream: a generic name for a road with a stream alongside it, as in the Washway at Enfield and Wash Lane in Peckham). But at no point did the Sewer Commissioners or anyone else use the name Effra. John Rocque on his 1746 map of London and Ten Miles Around marked its stream as 'The Shore' (a corruption of *sewer/shewer*). The tidal stretch between Kennington and the Thames became known as 'Vauxhall Creek' or occasionally 'Lambeth Creek' (see Plate 4A); further downstream it was 'the creek at Kennington Oval'. 'Brixton Washway' continued in use as the name for both road and river until the 1840s (See Plate 6A).

Perhaps the best evidence for the non-existence of the name Effra is found in Allen's history of Lambeth published in 1826 which includes a lengthy 'perambulation' of the parish describing its built and landscape features.[7] The Effra crops up repeatedly during the course of Allen's walkabout. He notes its mouth at Vauxhall and its stream by St Mark's Church in Kennington; he encounters it flowing along Brixton Road and in the south of the parish forming the boundary with Camberwell. Yet at no point does this Lambeth historian—who we must assume knew his local topography—use the name Effra. He refers to it variously as 'Vauxhall Creek', 'the creek at the other side of Cumberland Gardens', 'a stream' and 'a watercourse'. Nor, it seems, does he recognise that these are all instances of the same river.

Five years later, in 1831, the river name Effra is encountered for the first time when the Sewer Commissioners refer to the 'Vauxhall Creek or Effra Sewer behind Brixton Place' (the section of Brixton Road just by Coldharbour Lane). Following that chance usage the name is quickly adopted, at first just for that section of the river to the south of Coldharbour Lane, then for the whole river. Thirteen years later, when Edward Brayley published the third volume of his Surrey history, he could write confidently of the 'small stream called Effra… this rivulet takes its rise in the upper part of the Brixton district'.[8] Something clearly happened in between Allen's uncertainty and Brayley's confident description: a river which had previously had no single name suddenly became an entity.

In fact, the name Effra was being used slightly earlier in the eighteenth century, but as a place-name rather than as a way of denoting a river. In the 1790s, a seventy-acre holding

---

7   *History and Antiquities of the Parish of Lambeth*, Thomas Allen, 1826
8   *Topographical History of Surrey*, vol. III, 1844, p. 362

within the former Manor of Heathrow came up at auction; the land lay in Brixton to the south of Coldharbour Lane and was known as the 'Effra Farm' and the stream that would become known as the River Effra did flow through it,[9] hence that first use of 'Effra Sewer' by the Commissioners in 1831. When the Commissioners were required to define a particular stretch of the watercourse, they simply borrowed the name of the land it flowed through. In other words, Effra is a nineteenth-century 'back-formation'. The name does not come from any river-like attribute like 'torrent' or 'runlet of water', but simply from a place through which it flowed. And then, almost arbitrarily, the name sticks.[10]

Finally then, even if it is not a river name, where did the name Effra come from? The best suggestion to date is that it is a corruption of the name of the old Manor of Heathrow of which the farm was a part.[11] The manor disappeared in the seventeenth century whereupon the name ceased to be used, but in its sixteenth-century variant spellings, Hethdron and Hetherowe, one can just about trace the possibility of a corrupted descent into the word Effra.

A curious paradox about the Effra is that it had existed happily for centuries without a distinct name and then only acquired one just at the moment it started to vanish from sight. Its need for a name in the mid-nineteenth century, as the Metropolitan Commission of Sewers' surveyors fanned out along its length to measure its height and flow and extent, was part of the process of information management: coinciding as it did with the first attempt at a large-scale mapping of the city by the Ordnance Survey and with a growing sense of London as a metropolitan entity that now required definitive, rather than local, names. It was Bazalgette who would go on in the 1850s to give the Effra's two main streams their names: the 'Upper Norwood branch' and the 'Lower Norwood branch'.

In other words John Ruskin could not have got it more wrong. It was not just that his Latinate *Effrena* was impossible—never mind that the naming of the river only happened in his own youth. Far from locating some earlier, purer condition of untamedness, its new name was just one more aspect of its control and 'bridling' by the engineers of the Metropolitan Board of Works. For Ruskin, in the despair of his old age, it was one more intrusive intervention by the modern world—as the river that he had played in as a child and sketched as a young man was 'bricked over for the convenience of Mr Biffin, chemist, and others'.

---

9   *Survey of London*: Vol 26, Lambeth: Southern Area, 1956, p. 137
10 A reminder of the seemingly chance adoption of the name Effra is in *The Times* of 23 August 1876 when a woman living on Wandsworth Road referred to 'local traditions concerning the bed of the Effra, the Brix and their tributaries', suggesting that there were other local names in use.
11 *Effra; Lambeth's Underground River*, Ken Dixon, 1993

More recently South London has become accustomed to the renaming of its parts after they have undergone developer-led regeneration: the Oval Quarter rising from the ruins of the old Myatts Fields North housing estate and the 'estate-agent-friendly' transition of Granville Parade and Market Row into 'Brixton Village' come to mind. Is the adoption of the name Effra an early instance of this phenomenon? Did the pressure for a single coherent name also come from the middle-class owners of the houses recently constructed along its banks on Brixton Road and Kennington and in the new suburbs of Holland-Town and Angell-Town? Might they have yearned for the stream that flowed past their front doors to have slightly more social kudos than Vauxhall Creek or the Washway? Charles Dickens, who always had a sure touch for an area's sense of itself, located Mr Wilkins Flasher Esq. here in *Pickwick Papers* (1836-7): the wealthy stockbroker 'whose house was in Brixton, Surrey ... and who had a very open waistcoat, a very rolling collar, and very small boots, and very big rings, and a very large guard chain and a scented pocket handkerchief'. Maitland's history confirms the 'many suburban *Villas* and pleasant dwellings in this district, occupied by merchants and gentlemen of respectability and affluence'. The fictive Mr Flasher and his real neighbours along the Washway (which they succeeded in having renamed as Brixton Road in 1856) had been lobbying Sewer Commissioners, the local vestry and their MPs about the state of their river since the 1820s. Surely they at least welcomed its christening with such an historic-sounding name and would have been enthusiastic early adopters.

5

RIVER GODS AND RIVER MYTHS

The Celts understood rivers to be the bestowers of life and health and believed in river deities with healing powers. The remains of a huge oak bridge built 3,500 years ago that was excavated and identified in 1998 close to Vauxhall Bridge seems to support this. Like the ancient river ford at Battersea, some evidence of votive offerings found here suggests that it could have been a sacred site. So, two Bronze Age spearheads found by a 'mud lark' alongside the remains of the wooden structure may have been placed deliberately as a ritual offering. The Bronze Age shield dredged up at Battersea in the 1850s and the Iron Age helmet found at Waterloo Bridge a decade later may also be instances of this practice.

By the eighteenth and nineteenth centuries London's take on the idea of a river deity had declined down to Old Father Thames, a cosy fusion of a Classical bearded river god incorporating a nod to earlier local divinities like Gog and Magog, and which was suitable for a variety of commercial purposes: Coade-stone garden ornaments, a base design for cast iron lamp standards and the seal of a Lambeth water company. It was the closest to divinity that the metropolitan river was now going to get.

Old Father Thames reclines on his scallop shell before a
backdrop of Lambeth timber wharves and factories, 1785.

There have been no subsequent sightings of the Great God Pan on the River Effra along South Lambeth Road; Naiads have not been observed bathing in its stream at Herne Hill, nor Hamadryads found among the oaks of the Great North Wood. Yet this prosaic little stream that for many centuries was too obscure to even have a name, never mind a *genius loci*, certainly punches above its weight when it comes to river myths.

My father who grew up in East London used to walk as a child along the top of the Northern Outfall Sewer from Stratford to Barking. There, he told me, he would see wild tomatoes growing in profusion on the richly fertilised Thames foreshore mud beside the outfall. They had germinated there, he understood, from the partly digested seeds of salad tomatoes which had been eaten many miles away and which had passed through the guts of thousands of West Londoners before travelling the length of London's sewers to spill onto the mud of Barking Creek.

Like all good urban myths it was a story with just the right mix of the marginally plausible, the playfully imaginative and the ludicrous. It also has that element of concealment underground which is common to so many of these legends. My father's childhood was in the 1930s when the commercial growing of tomatoes under glass first turned a once exotic fruit into an affordable commonplace. It coincided, too, with the growth of allotment ownership and a better understanding of horticulture and the importance of fertilisers. He was a product of the London County Council's public education system which made sure that its schoolchildren learnt about the civic achievements of London's sewage system. One can begin to see how such a story might gain traction.

In the same vein there are many extraordinary and imaginative stories about the Effra that are still rehearsed and can be heard being heatedly argued over in pubs in South London. This chapter will look at three of them.

KING CANUTE SAILED UP THE RIVER EFFRA TO BRIXTON WITH HIS FLEET IN THE ELEVENTH CENTURY

This Effra story, which first emerged during the nineteenth century and which *The Times* was still playfully rehearsing in 1935,[1] conforms to a pattern by being patently untrue while also being based within attestable historic fact. In 1016, Canute, the King of Denmark and Norway, had attempted to capture Saxon London. His fleet of Viking longboats rowed up the Thames estuary but were blocked from getting into the city by the strongly fortified London Bridge. The subsequent events are recounted in the Anglo-Saxon Chronicle. 'Then came the ships to Greenwich[2], about the gang-days, and within a short interval went to London; where they sunk a deep ditch on the south side, and dragged their ships to the west side of the bridge.' Vikings were known for 'portaging' or dragging their boats overland to get around obstacles. London was surrendered later that year and Canute became King of England.

---

1   *The Times*, 1 March 1935
2   Deptford was called West Grenwyche in the Anglo-Saxon and medieval periods.

Tracing and defining the route that Canute's boats may have taken went on to become something of an antiquarian *cause célèbre* with writers like Daniel Defoe and Edward Maitland squabbling about whether the boats might have used the line of the Earl's Sluice, the Lock Stream or the Neckinger, and calculating the minimum turning circle of a Viking longboat to prove their point; a retired drainage engineer even worked out the likely water depth of flooded Bermondsey if the Vikings had a made a breach in the Thames wall.

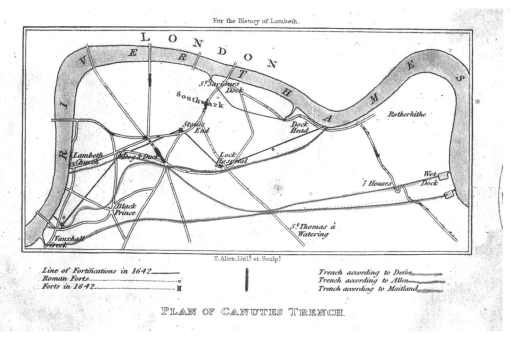

Thomas Allen was one of many London historians fascinated by the Canute story and he drew up this map in 1826 to show some of the possible routes the boats may have taken which include approximations of the courses of the Earl's Sluice and the Lock Stream.

Allen's plan shows some of the suggested possible routes for the trench across Southwark and Lambeth, one of these has the mouth of the Effra at Vauxhall Creek as Canute's point of re-entry into the Thames. However, the fanciful extension of the story which sees his long ships sailing up the Effra parallel with the Brixton Road, while delightful, was clearly impossible given the draught and width of his ships and, from Canute's point of view, strategically meaningless. Yet as we now know, if the course of the Earl's Sluice had been the route taken while passing round the back of London Bridge then the Viking boats would in fact have been dragged along the old course of the Effra—even though that information was not available to to earlier historians like Maitland and Allen.

DURING ONE OF THE EFFRA'S PERIODIC FLOODS A COFFIN INTERRED IN WEST NORWOOD CEMETERY WAS DISLODGED, DROPPED DOWN INTO THE EFFRA BENEATH AND WAS WASHED DOWNSTREAM INTO THE THAMES

Again, one can detect the little bit of factual grit that might have seeded this pearl of a story. The South Metropolitan Cemetery Company acquired the land in Norwood for the cemetery in 1836. The Effra did indeed flow across the cemetery's western corner and the company had quickly covered it over before opening in 1837, no doubt reasoning that a polluted stream with a tendency to flood would not sit well alongside their advertised product: a charmingly planted semi-rural burial space in which the Victorian middle classes might bury and discreetly mourn their dead. Adding to this story's plausibility is the fact that grave diggers at Norwood Cemetery report that burials do move about underground, particularly on a slope; they can open a plot and find that the coffin has eased its way out of its designated area and moved down the hill.

Between 1836 and 1862 the course of the river through the cemetery was covered over, but was not yet underground. After 1862 the Effra was diverted away from the cemetery altogether into a new sewer running along Norwood High Street. So the window for this particular story is just twenty-five years, but even then it is difficult to see how this could have happened as the Effra, although covered over, was still a surface stream that had not yet been buried underground. So it is difficult to envisage a coffin falling into it. After 1862, it was no longer flowing through the cemetery grounds.

Other possible outriders for this myth can be found in a couple of incidents from earlier in the nineteenth century. In May 1818, illustrating the potential body-carrying power of the Effra when in flood, *The Times* reported that 'while dragging the creek at Kennington in search of the body of James Simmonds, who was drowned in the late flood, a woman's bonnet and shawl, and a pair of men's shoes, were found, from which circumstances it is to be feared that some other persons were drowned that dreadful night; the flood being so very high, it is not unlikely that the bodies might have been carried by the strong current into the Thames where it empties itself.'[3] If the devastating floods of the Effra were capable of washing bodies downstream then this allowed for the extension of the idea to entire coffins.

In fact, dead bodies in sewers were already something of a recurrent motif. Henry Mayhew in *London Labour and London Poor* reports instances of sewer flushers going underground, being caught by the tide, and then their drowned bodies being eaten and reduced to skeletons by rats; the London press described the instance of one such skeleton found nibbled clean in a sewer beneath The Strand in 1840. The following year another story in *The Times* may have provided another prompt for the Norwood story: a skeleton was found seventy yards up the covered section of the Effra beyond Vauxhall Creek. It was first assumed a murder had taken place, but after a surgeon examined the bones, it was discovered that they were held together by wire and were probably the remains of a skeleton used for medical teaching. This prompted

---

3   *The Times*, 15 May 1818

The Times to huff, 'It is hardly possible to suppose that anyone could be so wanting in common decency to throw them into the Effra instead of burying them.'[4]

QUEEN ELIZABETH WOULD VISIT SIR WALTER RALEIGH AT HIS HOUSE IN BRIXTON BY SAILING UP THE EFFRA IN HER ROYAL BARGE

Perhaps we should not be surprised that into a long and busy reign (that included sleeping in more grateful subjects' beds and pausing to rest under more oak trees than any monarch before or since) Queen Elizabeth I also managed to fit at least two royal boat trips up the River Effra into her busy schedule. This enduring story, which many local people remember being told by their parents, continues to have a certain playful traction even today.

There are a number of variants depending on whether the tale was being told for a Brixton, a Herne Hill or a Dulwich audience. The earliest published account seems to be the one in Blanch's 1875 history of Camberwell which mentions a surviving ancient elm tree on Half Moon Lane: 'Queen Elizabeth, tradition says, took shelter beneath its noble boughs, whilst Edward Alleyn was no doubt an admirer of its majesty in his evening rambles through the woods.' Blanch then carefully alludes to Queen Elizabeth's royal progress up the River Effra as 'a local belief which it would perhaps be inadvisable to doubt'.[5]

By 1890 Blanch's fragmentary asides had coalesced into a story: Queen Elizabeth had sailed up the Effra from the Thames in her royal barge to visit Sir Edward Alleyn. Alleyn was indeed the owner of Dulwich Manor House and the Effra flowed close by it, but unfortunately he only acquired his Dulwich estate three years after the queen's death.[6] One tantalising explanation for the possible source of the mangled Elizabeth/Alleyn story relates to the new hall at Dulwich College, which when it opened in 1870 had transferred across to it an old wooden chimney piece from the original seventeenth-century college library. 'This curious chimney-piece … [was] constructed from a portion of Queen Elizabeth's state barge which Alleyn purchased when the barge was broken up in the reign of her successor.'[7] Is it this piece of quirky architectural salvage that provides the key to all of the subsequent Queen Elizabeth stories?

A Brixton version of the same royal progress emerged when the demolition of a large sixteenth-century house on Brixton Hill and the redevelopment of the site by speculative builders as Fairmount Road attracted a flurry of press interest. It was known that the Raleigh family had lived in the house known locally as Raleigh House in the past, so it was but a small leap to imagine that Sir Walter Raleigh had lived there despite there being no evidence for this. The demolition of the house in 1892 seems to have been the trigger for the emerging myth in local newspapers: 'it was certain that Queen Elizabeth had visited him there, coming up the now hidden Effra in her state barge'.[8]

---

4   *The Times*, 22 Sept 1841
5   *The Parish of Camberwell*, W.H. Blanch, 1875, pp. 408-9
6   *Norwood and Dulwich Past and Present*, A.M. Galer, 1890
7   Blanch *op. cit.*, p. 465
8   *The Penny Illustrated Paper*, 12 November 1892

The growth of the Brixton version was probably helped along by the close proximity of another sixteenth-century house on Brixton Hill. Ivy House stood by Blenheim Gardens just opposite Raleigh House and it survived long enough to be christened by Edwardian postcard photographers as 'Queen Elizabeth's House, Brixton Hill'. The fact that the two houses had been just about opposite one another allowed for the creation of a crucial sub-narrative in which an underground tunnel linked the two houses through which the lovers might secretly meet.

The geographical challenge of getting the royal barge up the narrow Effra, never mind getting the Effra to flow up the slope of Brixton Hill, is perhaps mitigated by a further confusion. In addition to Raleigh House on the hill, there was a regency house known as Raleigh Hall in the valley along Effra Road. It had no associations with the Raleigh family—and in fact now houses the Black Cultural Archives—but it did at least have the Effra flowing behind it.

Clearly the residents of Herne Hill must have been jealous of the regal attention their Brixton and Dulwich neighbours were receiving, and not wishing to miss out on the action, arrived at their own version of the story. If Elizabeth had penetrated up the Effra as far as Dulwich, then clearly she would have needed to rest under the shade of some agreeable tree or other on her route (as she had done elsewhere in South London at Honor Oak or One Tree Hill). A sufficiently old oak tree was unavailable, but a suitably ancient elm was found

*Queen Elizabeth's House,
Brixton Hill.*

Queen Elizabeth's House, Brixton Hill. The person sending this card wrote on the back in 1907: 'You can see this house from the High Road. It is in great disrepair. Quite near Sir W[alter] Raleigh used to have a house and go up the River Effra in his barge to London.'

PLATE 1. The Ambrook on Sydenham Hill, one of the uncovered tributaries of the Effra, photo David Western, 2016

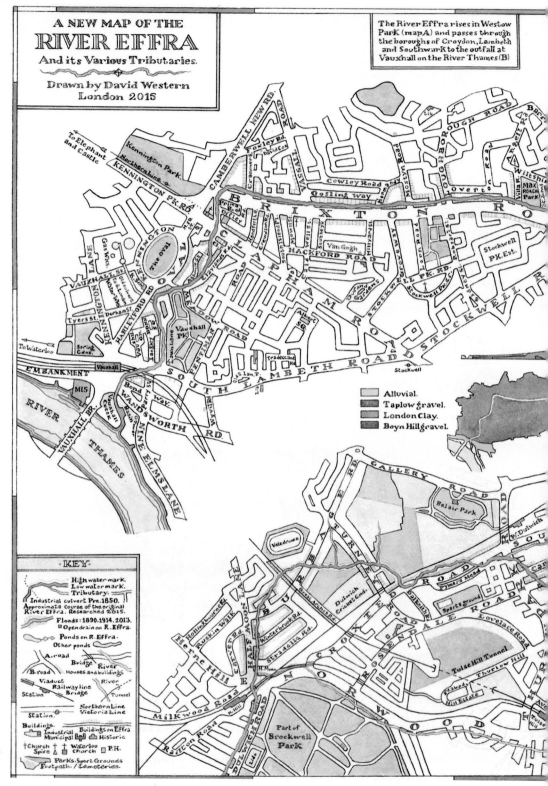

PLATE 2 and 3. "A New Map of the River Effra", watercolour, ink and gouache, David Western, 201⁵

B. Effra North

Flood plain gravel.
Clay gate bed.

Geological map of the Effra river valley.

N

A. Effra South

1 Kilometre

PLATE 4A. Vauxhall Creek, watercolour wash, J Skinner, 1783

PLATE 4B. South London Waterworks at Kennington, which took its water from the Effra at Vauxhall Creek, oil painting, anon., ca 1815

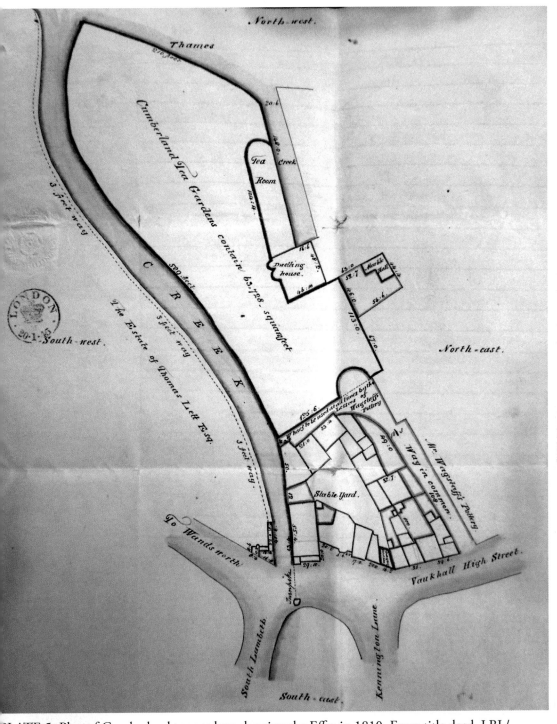

PLATE 5. Plan of Cumberland tea gardens showing the Effra in 1810. From title deed, LBL/DALS/7/4/5 (LAD)

PLATE 6A. Brixton Road with the Effra flowing beside it, col. engraving, 1783

PLATE 6B. Herne Hill looking north from Norwood Road to the entrance to Brockwell Hall and the Half Moon Lane bridge over the Effra, col. lithograph, 1823

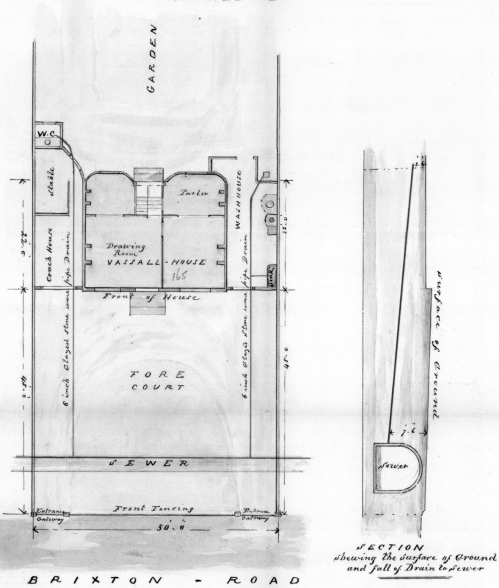

PLATE 7. Plan of Vassall House, Brixton Road, showing drainage into the Effra in front of the
house, 1856. LBL/DCEPS/DRG/977 (LAD)

PLATE 8A. The Half Moon at Herne Hill, watercolour, ink and gouache, David Western, 2016

PLATE 8B. Replacement of concrete paving at Rosendale Allotments so that the soil absorbs and stores storm water run-off, photo London Wildlife Trust

in the grounds of Elm Lodge at Half Moon Lane (as Blanch had mentioned in 1875). It stood conveniently beside the Effra and in 1927, when it was threatened with being felled, local artists and the national press rushed to record its imminent disappearance and to make the historical links. *The Sunday Times* estimated it to be more than 300 years old and that its massive trunk, 'would entirely fill the front garden of an average suburban villa.'[9]

All the versions of the Queen Elizabeth story have a number of things in common. They all post-date the disappearance of the Effra underground and each of them is linked with a local historic feature at the moment when it - be it an old house, a college building or an ancient tree - is changed, threatened or demolished. It was Walter Besant who in 1898 declared, 'We have not only destroyed the former beauty of South London: we have forgotten it' (although it might just as easily have been the nostalgic Ruskin). In each of these stories, confronted by the destruction of an older landscape and its historical associations, the link with the invisible Effra becomes one means of holding onto a vanishing sense of place. It becomes a way of creating a geographical and narrative thread to connect up with what was seen as a larger and more tangible national history of kings and queens and London, one that would endow these local fragments with significance and authenticity. In that sense the choice of narrative connector, a river that has itself also been removed from sight and increasingly from memory, feels rather appropriate regardless of the underlying absurdity of the stories.

---

9   *The Sunday Times*, 28 March 1927

6

FUTURE EFFRA

In 1899 Joseph Bazalgette's memorial was unveiled on London's Victoria Embankment. It is a bronze portrait bust set in a low Portland stone arcade that looks across to Northumberland Avenue. It bears the inscription *Flumini Vincula Posuit*: a grand assertion, but not an overstated one for this moral, stable-cleansing Hercules of Victorian London. After all, this was the man who had diverted its rivers into his intercepting sewers, who had contained the Thames within the Victoria, Albert and Chelsea Embankments and who had bridged it by building or re-building Hammersmith, Putney, Battersea and the Albert Bridges. He might indeed, without fear of hubris, claim to have 'put chains on the rivers'

And yet it is arguable that if a twenty-first-century Bazalgette were called upon to re-engineer the Effra 150 years on, then things would be done very differently. Temperamentally we are becoming more sympathetic to Ruskin's idea of an unbridled river than to Bazalgette's notion of a chained one. And this is not just sentiment. Increasingly 'soft' engineering solutions are being looked to as the way to manage rivers—particularly when confronted by the prospect of rising water levels caused by climate change as well as by some recent high-profile failures of older, 'hard' engineering solutions—whether the raised levees along the Mississippi that contributed to the catastrophic flooding of New Orleans in 2005 or the way that the straightened and channelled rivers of the UK accelerate river flooding. There is increasing recognition that you cannot totally design a river away, that you have to work with its force.

One thread in the discussions around soft engineering solutions is the notion that rivers once consigned underground might be reinstated on the surface. In California in the San Francisco Bay Area this has led to the reopening of tributaries of the Sacramento and San Joaquin rivers long buried in concrete pipes. Within London, following on from the Environment Agency's 2009 River Restoration programme, there has been a flurry of suggestions for uncovering underground streams. The best South London example can be seen on the River Quaggy, a tributary of the Ravensbourne, at Sutcliffe Park in Kidbrooke where a previously straight underground section has been de-culverted, re-meandered and has had reed beds and back waters created as habitats for wildlife. As well as creating a more attractive landscape the pooling and slowing of the river's flow diminishes the risk of flooding further downstream.

As the Metropolitan Board of Works discovered way back in the 1870s, the more you build on the Thames basin, the more you increase the risk of surface water and flash flooding. That problem has not diminished; on the contrary it is now estimated that an area of green space equivalent to the size of two and a half Hyde Parks is lost annually in London to paving in private gardens alone. Germany and the Netherlands have long had policies requiring systems for the retention of storm water on the land where it falls. In 2014, ten years after the disastrous floods in Dulwich and Herne Hill of April 2004, when two and a half inches of rainfall fell over two hours and flooded more than 200 properties, the Herne Hill and Dulwich Flood Alleviation Scheme was completed using these principles. Underground storage areas were constructed in Dulwich Park, Dulwich Sports Ground and Belair Park to capture and store surface and storm water and then release it after peak flows had subsided. The scheme also created wetlands and wildflower meadows as wildlife habitat. A similar approach is being explored for re-using the length of the abandoned sewer beneath Norwood Cemetery as underground storage for surface water.

Another innovation in the Effra catchment area, London Wildlife Trust's Lost Effra project, uses soft engineering solutions to alleviate flooding caused by rainfall. These local initiatives have included the creation of 'rain gardens' at Cressingham Gardens to absorb and use the water from downpipes that would have previously flowed away as surface run-off, the restoration of natural wetlands in the headwater catchments on Sydenham Hill to slow and control water descending into the Effra valley (see Plate 1), and the removal of concrete and tarmac areas to increase natural drainage of surface water. Some 180 square yards of concrete was removed from the entrance at Rosendale community allotments on the hillside above the high flood risk areas of Dulwich; by replacing this with cellular paving it can now store storm water run-off instead of sending it as surface water down into Dulwich (See Plate 8B).

While the Effra's upper headwaters are still to be seen, there is little likelihood of the main river being uncovered again: it was too comprehensively built over too early on. Instead, we must content ourselves with clues and glimpses. The ghost of the Effra still possesses the streets—you can still hear its waters below manholes along the upper river. You can still see its valley cutting through the suburban street lines of Norwood or passing between gaps in the houses. You can still follow the line of stink pipes (the high cast-iron pipes installed to vent sewer gas) along Dulwich Road or the row of elevated manholes behind Hanover Gardens.

Bazalgette believed he had made the Effra vanish for the greater good, but for many South Londoners living along its underground course or above one of its tributaries, the river is inescapably there. Some things just do not go away: the curious marshy patches in Kennington Park, the house that collapsed at Thurlow Park Road, the constant standing water in the car breakers' yard in Windsor Grove, the flood surges up the back gardens of Dulwich Road, the mysterious clear water in the flooded basements of Railton Road, the constant flooding of Clive Road in the 1970s, the swamping of Turney Road in 2004…

For all the accumulated engineering expertise of the Board of Works and its successors, most recently Thames Water, the risk of failure in a highly engineered system is inescapable. The river will still out. Every now and again, in an unbridled moment, the Effra will rise from its sewers—perhaps to the grim satisfaction of the ghost of John Ruskin.

AN ITINERARY OF THE RIVER

This itinerary, used alongside the map (Plates 2 and 3), provides a walkers' guide for anyone wishing to follow the routes of the two principal branches of the Effra (the Lower Norwood and the Upper Norwood) from their sources along the main stream of the river to its mouth into the Thames at Vauxhall. There is also a suggested walking route for those completionists wanting to try and follow the probable pre-medieval course of the river to the Thames at Rotherhithe.

THE LOWER NORWOOD BRANCH

This stream rises on the slope just south of Church Road, Upper Norwood, in what is now Westow Park. The hummocky surface of the ground is almost certainly caused by 'spring-sapping', which along with the steep slopes of the park is very suggestive of a river's headwater territory. In 2016 one of these source springs, fenced by chestnut palings, could still be seen in the park leaking, rather than flowing, down the hill from between a cluster of drain covers.

Westow Park.

The stream flows south down the park and along the line of Chevening Road to cross Hermitage Road before disappearing into the grounds of Virgo Fidelis Convent School. This institution, founded as a Catholic orphan school by a group of French nuns in the 1840s, initially for Irish victims of the potato famine, moved to its Norwood site in 1857. The original Georgian house which the nuns occupied and renamed St Mary's Lodge had been built as the private residence for Augustus Hervey, the Earl of Bristol, and his partner Mary Nesbit; they had acquired a modest and lonely rural cottage on 'a space of cleared land enclosed from Norwood Common' in the 1780s and had it rebuilt into a grander house. The cleared land was laid out as gardens and a former gravel pit through which the Effra flowed became 'a poplar-girded pond'. By the 1840s it was a private hotel, The Park Hotel, but crossed by public footpaths. After the convent acquired it the grounds were fenced in and access was lost. A visitor to Virgo Fidelis in the 1960s recalled being shown 'one room where they have a trap door and when this was raised it revealed standing, clean, odour-less water at 2-3' below floor level'.

The Effra descending through the remains of Norwood Common, now Norwood Park. The fenced grounds of Virgo Fidelis Convent can be seen behind, ca. 1860.

The river then flows south out of the convent grounds, under a bridge beneath Central Hill (a pinch point that frequently flooded after heavy rain) just to the west of the junction with Elder Road and then heading north-west, crosses under Elder Road to angle across Norwood Park.

Norwood Park, created in 1911, preserves a fragment of old open land, although the line of the Effra flowing through it once marked a more ancient landscape boundary. To the west had lain the poor unenclosed lands of Norwood Common, a rough open space once used for grazing but which was turned into building plots after the enclosure of Lambeth Manor in 1806. The large rectangle of land bounded by Central Hill, Knights Hill Road, Chapel and Gipsy Roads and Elder Road became a grid of streets, leaving just this small section of common east of Elder Road. To the west of the Effra in Norwood Park, again until 1806, had stood the oak woods of Clayland Coppice and Great Elder Hole Coppice, the northernmost of the Archbishops of Canterbury woodlands comprising the Great North Wood, which had extended north as far as Norwood Cemetery.

Norwood Park.

On a long site along the west side of Elder Road are the remains of the former Lambeth Children's Workhouse, subsequently known as Woodvale, and home among many thousands of other children to the young Charlie Chaplin. A gate house, some brick walls, railings and gateposts are all that remains of that 'assemblage of pompous buildings that are eloquent of the spread of poverty'.[1] The workhouse was frequently flooded by the Effra and a white stone tablet high up on the former relieving office wall, now removed, marked the line of the July 1890 flood. Even this far upstream the Effra was polluted: in 1859 Lambeth Vestry had noted its 'foul condition and its contaminating influence upon the atmosphere [that] must seriously endanger the health of the children in the school'.

The stream runs north across Norwood Park to bisect Norwood Park Road and Eylewood Road, both laid out in 1939 after the rest of the area had already been developed. Both roads cross the deep and visible valley of the Effra, perhaps one of the reasons they were built so late. The line of the Effra can be clearly seen, doglegging through wider gaps between the houses. Along Gipsy Road the river valley is also visible and the stink pipe at the lowest point, erected in 1863 when Bazalgette was sinking the stream into the 'Effra Branch sewer', just confirms the point.

The valley of Gipsy Road in 1925.

From Gipsy Road the West End and Crystal Palace Railway between West Norwood and Gipsy Hill stations follows the river valley running north between Auckland Hill and Norwood High Street. The line was built in 1857 when the company culverted the stream here. Before the

1   *Norwood in Days of Old*, W.T. Philips, 1912

railway was built, the Effra at this point is shown on old maps as a long wide stretch of water with an island which was known as 'The Reservoir', possibly once an ornamental water feature.

Windsor Grove.

Between Auckland Hill and the wall of Norwood Cemetery is a low-lying area of land. In the early nineteenth century this had been Elm Grove, a large detached house and grounds. After the cemetery opened in 1837 and walled out the view it must have become less desirable as a residence; it was briefly converted into a boarding school before being demolished and replaced by the smaller-scale houses of Wood Street and Dunbar Place in the 1860s. Walk into Dunbar Street today and a few of these still survive along with the little brick Bethel Chapel. Most were demolished and replaced in 1977 with a compact, low-rise small estate development. Drop down the slope to the Effra at the bottom and just at the lowest point where Dunbar Street curves to become Dunelm Grove is a small public garden backed by the cemetery wall. Here the Effra flowed through into the cemetery grounds.

This low-lying spot was also the point where another smaller tributary flowing east from Knights Hill joined the stream and it was always a vulnerable location prone to flooding. The local Norwood historian, Wilson, describing the flood here on 14 June 1914, wrote of 'Sunday joints being washed out of ovens' and the homeless having to sleep the night in a public hall on Knights Hill.

The Wood Street flood of 1914, now Dunelm Grove.

When the South Metropolitan Cemetery Company acquired the land for their cemetery in 1836 the Effra flowed through the grounds. A polluted stream with a tendency to flood did not sit easily with the company's prospectus for a pastoral garden enclave for the burial of the dead and they quickly covered it over. The outline of its valley can still be seen flowing north-south across the cemetery from Dunbar Street to Robson Road. As part of the construction of the Effra Branch sewer in the 1860s the stream was diverted out of the cemetery into a sewer running to the west along Norwood High Street, rejoining the old course above Chestnut Road. After this drainage system was built the stretch of river between Chestnut Road and Herne Hill was the only part of the Effra that remained in sight, although it no longer had much water in it. The photographs of its willow-edged water meadows, looking south-east over the street line of Lancaster Road towards Rosendale Road and Crystal Palace, were taken by a local photographer in the 1870s just before the houses of Idmiston Road, Chatsworth Way and Ardlui Road were built across the valley. So complete was the process of suburbanisation that this view can now barely be imagined.

The water meadows of the Effra, ca 1870.

To follow an approximation of the course of the river across its former meadows turn into Chatsworth Way and keeping its church on your left, descend Idmiston Road to cross the river valley and then ascend to the corner of Tulsemere Road. Here because of the bend the river makes, one has two views of the Effra valley: one back down Idmiston Road and the other looking down Tulsemere Road. Go into Tulsemere Road, then turn right onto Eastmearn Road, cross Rosendale Road and follow Carson Road round to reach Thurlow Park Road. This is the point the Lower Norwood branch meets with the Upper Norwood branch just north of Thurlow Park Road and west of Croxted Road, roughly behind the playground of Oakfield Preparatory School.

Ardlui Road.

THE UPPER NORWOOD BRANCH

This stream rose adjacent to Vicar's Oak, a single large tree last seen standing in the late seventeenth century that stood on the high point marking the parish boundaries between Bromley, Penge, Croydon, Lambeth and Camberwell (and today marks the boundaries of the boroughs of Lambeth, Southwark, Croydon and Bromley). Major civil engineering works carried out here in the 1850s —the re-erection of the Great Exhibition building as the Crystal Palace on the south side of Crystal Palace Parade and the cutting through of the Crystal Palace

51

High Level railway on the north side—meant that the river must have been culverted then. It is shown on plans of the 1860s emerging from under the station (the brick retaining walls constructed to hold its deep cutting in place are still to be seen on the north side of Crystal Palace Parade) before making an improbable 180-degree turn into Farquhar Road. The line of nos. 1-13 Farquhar Road follows the line of the stream as it curves sharply around their back gardens. From Farquhar Road into Jasper Road the river is marking the old Lambeth/Camberwell parish boundary; the dip of the stream by an old boundary post can be seen where it crosses Jasper Passage. It rapidly descends the hill, following the railway line after it emerges from its tunnel, then crossing under it at the point where Woodland Street curves back to Gipsy Hill. The stream passes under Colby Road (the dip in the road visible just beyond the Colby Arms pub) and under Dulwich Wood Avenue to then run down a long triangle of open ground known variously as Bell Meadow, Hunter's Meadow or French's Field (after the cow keeper who grazed his animals there in the early twentieth century and whose cowsheds on Cawnpore Street still survive as workshops).

Bell Meadow previously known as French's Field.

Cows grazing in French's Field, ca 1890.

Rejoining Gipsy Hill at the junction with Dulwich Wood Park, it passes south under the roundabout and along Paxton Place, the mews at the side of the Paxton Hotel which originally provided its stabling, before joining and following the line of South Croxted Road.

As well as marking the boundary between Lambeth and Southwark on the west side of the road, the river along South Croxted Road also defines the edge of the Dulwich Estate. There is a uniform feel to the estate's decent, unostentatious houses that line the road here, built in the 1890s of London stock brick with high gables, flat-fronted bays and modest red-brick decoration, and with the Effra marking the limit of their territory at the bottom of their back gardens.

Close to the junction of Hamilton and Clive Roads another stream joined it from the slope of Salters Hill—an area remembered in the 1840s as a 'a swampy flat stretching towards Dulwich' approached by a 'footpath which, like a causeway, ran above the low lying adjacent land' and where the writer remembered seeing gipsy tents.[2] Bazalgette tidied up the kinks and deviations of the original stream in the 1860s, so as a culverted sewer it now runs north in a

---

2   *Norwood in Days of Old*, W.T. Philips, 1912

Paxton Place.

straight line beside South Croxted Road and its continuation as Croxted Road for almost a mile and a half. At the junction with Thurlow Park Road the Upper Norwood branch unites with the Lower Norwood branch.

THE MAIN RIVER

This junction of the Upper Norwood and Lower Norwood streams just north of Thurlow Park Road and to the west of Croxted Road was the point at which Bazalgette created the most southerly of his intercepting sewers, the Effra Branch Sewer, which siphoned off much of the river's flow underground to drive the sewage of Norwood, Dulwich and Nunhead out to the Southern Outfall at Crossness. At this point the waters of the Effra dropped eight feet down a thirty-foot concrete run to disappear into its closed brick sewer.

It was here, in the 1820s, along what had previously been Croxted Lane, that John Ruskin used to play as a child in the Effra's 'tadpole haunted ditch'. The lane retained its rural feel for a few years after the river had vanished, but the removal of the stream underground undoubtedly contributed to the ease with which the land each side of it could then be developed. As an old man in the 1880s Ruskin grieved at what had become of it. 'The fields on each side of it are now mostly dug up for building, or cut through into gaunt corners and nooks of blind ground by the wild crossings and concurrencies of three railroads. Half a dozen handfuls of new cottages, with Doric doors, are dropped about here and there among the gashed ground: the lane itself, now entirely grassless, is a deep-rutted, heavy-hillocked cart-road, diverging gatelessly into various brick-fields or pieces of waste.'[3]

Croxted Lane ca. 1870.

The line of the river continues north along Croxted Road as far as Dalkeith Road where it turns west and passes under the railway line to loop around Dulwich. Seven years after Ruskin had mourned the vanishing of Croxted Lane a local journalist added his lament for a vanished rural

3   *Praeterita*, John Ruskin, vol. 1, 1884, p. 100; *Fors Clavigera*, 1882

idyll. 'It appears to be the making of Croxted Road that has diverted the water from flowing under the arch of the [railway] embankment into the Dulwich meadows. There should be a tablet put up "Under this arch, from 1862-1890, flowed the River Effra, a stream that flowed its way through meadow lands".'[4]

This was the very last section of the river to be built over. In 1891 the future was in plain sight and a poignant report in the *South London Press* anticipates its disappearance. 'Only some half mile of its wanderings can now be followed … through a valley of level pasture not yet handed over to the builder. He is however conspicuously invited, and plane-planted roads with sewers beneath are ready for him. Till his actual advent cricket, lawn tennis and football clubs are temporary tenants… Its course can readily be observed through the meadows spoken of, for even the parts filled in are not yet covered with grass and in some places the willows indicate it. Many of the little tributary streams can also be traced. One of the newly laid roads is named Turney Road.'[5]

In fact the suburban development of Dulwich, under the watchful eye of the Dulwich Estate, was much less of a free-for-all land grab than what had happened earlier along the Effra valley at Norwood and Brixton, and many of the former meadows are still at least playing

Dulwich playing fields.

4   *South London Press*, 29 August 1891
5   *South London Press*, 29 August 1891

fields. The housing development along Turney Road and Burbage Road feels only skin-deep. The railway lines (the Effra crosses again under the line at Great Arches Road) and the green open spaces of Dulwich College's and Alleyn's sports grounds, the Velodrome and Belair Park, have all impeded the house builder so that, although out of sight, the Effra here still largely runs through 'green fields' before returning into Lambeth along Half Moon Lane.

Great Arches Road.

Along Turney and Burbage Roads a couple of smaller tributaries join the stream from the west; one of these, the Ambrook coming from Sydenham Hill, was also joined by a stream that used to descend from the lake in Belair Park. The Effra then aligns itself with Half Moon Lane, flowing west along the tops of Winterbrook and Stradella Roads and under the Herne Hill

Baptist Church and the Half Moon pub to the junction with Norwood Road and the railway at Herne Hill (See Plates 6A & 8A).

Herne Hill Baptist Church.

Once again, John Ruskin is the source for a description of the earlier Effra stream. His family lived in a house on the top of Herne Hill and it was here that Ruskin recalled coming to make one of his earliest adolescent sketches in the 1830s of 'a view of the bridge over the now bricked-up Effra by which the Norwood Road then crossed it at the bottom of Herne Hill; the road itself, just at the place where from the top of the bridge, one looked up and down the streamlet, bridged now into putridly damp shade by the railway, close to Herne Hill Station.'[6] (See Plate 6B).

At Herne Hill, after turning west to pick its way under the railway line by the station and across the bottom of Railton Road, the stream cuts along an alley to reach the north side of Dulwich Road beside what was the Brockwell Park Tavern and is now The Florence. Two houses west of the alley and down from the pub is 129 Dulwich Road where Mr Biffin (the butt of Ruskin's Effra jibe, 'recently, I regret to say, bricked over for the convenience of Mr Biffin, chemist, and others') had his chemist's shop. Ruskin, writing in the 1880s, had an old

6   *Praeterita*, vol. 1, p. 87

man's sense of 'recently': the new sewer had actually been laid over twenty years earlier.[7] Biffin was presumably one of the Dulwich Road residents who had urged the Metropolitan Board of Works to get the work done. Given that his shop was just by the point where the stream turned after flowing through the alley it must have been particularly vulnerable to flooding.

The alley running between Railton Road and Norwood Road.

As one walks into Dulwich Road, once called Water Lane, there is still a sense of entering into a river valley. This was the gap in the hills through which the Effra had to flow to reach the Thames and to the south the slope of Brockwell Park climbs up the flank of Knights Hill; while to the north, behind the cyclopean Nissen hut that is Meath House, can be seen the heights of Herne Hill; west along Dulwich Road a line of stink pipes way-marks the former river's course along the valley floor. Further down Dulwich Road the Prince Regent pub, first built in the 1830s, was originally accessed by a small wooden bridge over the Effra's stream.

7   MBW/2426/33, contracts register, (LMA)

Brixton Water Lane.

At Brixton Water Lane another tributary joins the Effra before it flows along the line of Dalberg Road into what was once the Effra Farm Estate. The fate of Effra Hall (the original house, not the later pub) is a useful symbol for Brixton's decline in social status during the nineteenth century. The 'Hall', probably built after 1824 when the old farm estate was broken up, was an attractive detached villa with the Effra sparkling through its grounds. However, such was the failure of Brixton as a fashionable suburb that by the 1840s the Hall had become an asylum 'for ladies nervously or mentally afflicted'. As private mental health care of the time went it claimed to be of the best quality, providing 'padded and other apartments as to render mechanical restraint in the worst cases unnecessary, affording classification to the insane, quietude to the nervous, and to the epileptic, those accommodations which are so particularly required' (a euphemism that may refer to the use of straitjackets). It catered for twenty women living in the house and on a ward in the grounds until closing in 1873.

Once the Effra Diversion Sewer was laid out in 1862-63, the river no longer ran through Effra Hall so there was potentially more money to be made out of property speculation than from mental illness. The house builders of the Effra Hall Estate, as the area became known, ran the modest terraces of Saltoun, Kellett and Mervan Roads at right-angles across the now-

Effra Hall when in use as a private asylum, ca 1850.

dry river valley. The Hall was demolished (it had stood just back from Effra Road opposite St Matthews' Church, roughly on the site of nos. 1-5 and 2-6 Kellett Road), so it was only fitting that the new pub built in the then-fashionable Victorian 'Egyptian' style on the corner of Kellett and Rattray Roads should perpetuate the name as the Effra Hall Tavern.

Effra Hall Tavern.

Dalberg Road.

Beyond the Effra Hall estate, the river flows north under the junction of Vining Street and Rushcroft Road to Coldharbour Lane—the shallow dip in the road where the stream crosses can still just be discerned—before passing beneath Connaught Mansions and Market Row, crossing Atlantic Road and then aligning with Pope's Road and Canterbury Crescent to arrive at Brixton police station.

Brixton's ability to develop into a suburban town centre must have been hampered by the presence of an open muddy stream flowing through its centre. The solution was the Effra Diversion Sewer, which rerouted the Effra from Dulwich Road to run along Brixton Water Lane, then north onto Effra Road, past St Matthew's Church and Windrush Square to reach Brixton Road where it re-joined the course of the old river outside the police station.[8] This rerouting onto main roads and the filling in of the original course, completed by 1863, enabled both the Effra Hall estate development of the 1870s and the later Brixton Markets development in the 1880s. The diversion sewer along Effra Road also encouraged the misconception that Effra Road was named after the river when in fact its naming pre-dated that of the river and derives from the laying out of Effra Farm after 1808.

---

8   MBW/2426/30, contracts register, (LMA)

Pope's Road.

By the side of Brixton police station running down the line of Canterbury Crescent there is still a sense of the Effra's shallow river valley. This stretch had been covered over in 1857 by the Metropolitan Board of Works but the benefit was short-lived as five years later it was no longer required; after the diversion sewer rerouted the river along Brixton Road the course along Canterbury Crescent was filled in.[9]

From Brixton police station the river runs north along the east side of Brixton Road. This section of the river and the road were both known as the Washway until the 1840s (from the Old English *Waesse*, a swamp, with the derived sense of 'a stream'). House owners here fought a long battle with the Commissioners of Sewers between 1820 and 1850 to get the stream in front of their gardens covered over. The northern section of the river from Mostyn Road up to Kennington had been 'arched over' in the 1820s but it was not until 1847, after much lobbying and complaining, that the Commissioners did the same for the southern section between Mostyn Road and the police station.

One of the arguments for covering over the river was for the occupants of the new suburbs being built on the east side to have access to the main road; the other was to conceal the sight and

9   MBW/2426/02, contracts register, (LMA)

mask the smell of its increasingly polluted waters. Brixton Road residents complained regularly about the sewage draining into the stream from houses upriver (see page 17), but at the same time they were happy to add their own contributions to the public health problem as it was standard practice for these houses to pipe their own waste directly into the river (See Plate 7).

The rebuilt White Horse pub on Brixton Road is now the Brixton Jamm, but when it was a coaching inn it had been almost the only building along the lonely eighteenth-century turnpike road (See Plate 6A). It was subject to regular inundations, and in 1818 the landlord, William Tinkler, drowned when the Effra flooded after extremely heavy rain (see page 27).[10] It is at the White Horse that the second of Bazalgette's 'intercepting' sewers, the Southern High Level running from Clapham to the outfall at Crossness, crosses the Effra, doglegging from

Brixton Road at Vassall Road.

10   *The Times*, 12-17 May 1818

Robsart Street into Loughborough Road and increasing its width from six feet to nine feet to accommodate the river's flow.

Traces of the Effra can still be seen along the length of Brixton Road. The extra roadway in front of Angell Terrace beyond the police station, the belts of parkland between Villa Road and Loughborough Road, the way that Regency survivors like Peckford Place are set so well back from the road line, the extended front gardens of the terraces between Mostyn Road and Normandy Road, and the ornamental beds with trees in front of the houses between Vassall and Cranmer Roads: all of these are reminders that a river once flowed here, and the building line had been set well back, respected by Georgian developers and the builders of post-war council flats alike.

At the top of Brixton Road, where the Effra was diverted in the thirteenth century to turn west, the river flows under the roadway at Hazard's Bridge (from Hazard's Marsh, the earlier name for this low-lying area) into Prima Road to reach Clapham Road. In doing so it flows in front of a low mound occupied in succession by two strikingly different institutions. The Kennington gallows stood here from the late seventeenth century; prisoners were brought by cart from Kingston and Croydon courthouses to be ogled by enthusiastic crowds on public hanging days. The last execution took place in 1799 and just 25 years later St Mark's Church

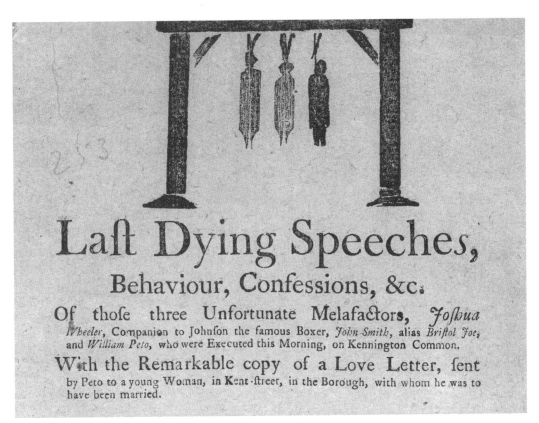

Execution handbill for Kennington gallows, eighteenth century.

for the new parish of Kennington was built on the site. When digging its foundations, the workmen uncovered one of the gibbet irons used for screwing into the skulls of executed prisoners prior to their being hung in chains. When the church was planned the vestry had sought to have the river along Prima Road (previously Church Road) 'arched' over, anticipating the incongruity of a burial ground bordered by a polluted stream, but only finally came up with the money for the work in 1838.[11]

Prima Road by St Mark's churchyard.

After flowing under Clapham Road at Merton Bridge (its upkeep had been the responsibility of Merton Abbey while Hazard's Bridge had been that of Bermondsey Abbey), the Effra passes above the Northern Line and between Oval tube station and the north side of Hanover Gardens, continuing behind the backs of Rothesay Court and Oval House and curving around the houses on the north-east side of Hanover Gardens. The whirligig of time and of London property prices has been at play here. Given these houses' current desirability, it is interesting to contrast the view from 1849 when their modest early nineteenth-century terraces, squeezed by the line of the stream into an asymmetric square, were the subject of an urgent sanitary

11   SKCS/65, minutes; SKCS/136, contracts, (LMA)

report which found 'loud complaints' being made about the Effra at the 'north side of Hanover Place. The houses in the latter mentioned are of the third class closely built and fully or over-tenanted and abutting as they do on the sewer, soil and all other matters upon them are carried into it thereby rendering it a nuisance of the most dangerous kind. Several deaths have indeed lately occurred from low fever in this poor and crowded spot.'[12] Eight years later, in 1857, the residents were still petitioning Lambeth Vestry about the river's 'foul condition and offensive character' but it was another three years before the £300 was found for covering the stream 'at the rear of Harleyford Street and Hanover Place and along to the garden of Rose Lawn cottage [now Oval tube station]'.[13]

Lawn Lane.

---

12   *St Mark's district sanitary report*, 1849, P3/75/7 (LAD)
13   Lambeth Sewers Committee, November 1860, P3/139/1 (LAD)

From Hanover Gardens the Effra picks its way across the Triangle adventure playground, passes between the Roebuck pub and the rear of Archbishop Tenison's school, flows beneath one wing of Stoddart House and then in between Shrewsbury and Wisden Houses before passing from the public space of the Ashmole Estate into the private, gated zone of Bedser Close. (To follow its course it is necessary to go back around Ashmole Place and Claylands Road.) Until the seventeenth century, the river divided into two streams at this point; the right-hand one, now vanished, flowed along the line of Harleyford Road to Vauxhall, the left-hand stream turning sharply at Bedser Close to flow west along the line of Ebbisham Drive, passes between the high-rise of Bannerman House and the back gardens of Bonnington Square, to follow the line of Lawn Lane to South Lambeth Road. Bonnington Square and Ebbisham Drive used to be an area of market gardens that was watered by the Effra until the 1860s. After the river went into its underground sewer the market gardener, Mr Alderson, complained about his loss of irrigation (see page 27).

The river's course along this stretch is a succession of right-angled bends which originally followed or created field and estate boundaries. In the late eighteenth century when John Fentiman acquired them, the lands here were marshland. Fentiman persevered and 'having drained the ground and filled up the hollows at a considerable expense, enclosed several acres for plantations and pleasure grounds and built a handsome mansion for his own abode'.[14] His house and grounds were acquired by The Little Sisters of the Poor in 1861. The 'mansion' was rebuilt in the 1980s but still function as a Catholic care home for the elderly: St Peter's Residences.

The course of the river goes around the south-west edge of The Oval, once known as 'Sluice House Field', a name which helps to explain why in densely occupied Kennington it was never built on. The tides from the Thames came up the Effra to this point, and even after Surrey Cricket Club took it as their ground in 1845 it continued to suffer from flooding. In October 1860 the ground was under water and 'notwithstanding the best exertions were used, it was not until the third tide after the flooding that The Oval ground was relieved of the water from its surface'.[15] This was also the location of the South London Water Works' reservoir fed by the Effra on what is now the gasworks site to the north of The Oval (See Plate 4B).

At South Lambeth Road where the Effra turns north there was another tidying up of the stream in the seventeenth century. Previously this stream had crossed South Lambeth Road and continued west to a second mouth into the Thames at Nine Elms Lane. This was filled in and a new cut run along South Lambeth Road to Cox's Bridge on the Wandsworth Road. South of this point stood The Lawn, a grand Georgian terrace since demolished for Vauxhall Park, which had a small lake in front of it fed by the Effra. In 1835 one of its occupants, Henry Puckle, complained vociferously about the pestilential pollution from the river. Pestilential and disgusting it may have been but that did not prevent later residents of The Lawn from unsuccessfully petitioning the Metropolitan Board of Works for compensation for loss of amenity after the Board had drained away their ornamental water in 1864.

---

14   Brayley vol. III, 1847, p. 363
15   Lambeth Sewers Committee, 1860, P3/139/1 (LAD)

South Lambeth Place.

The construction of the railway line from Nine Elms in to Waterloo in 1847 tidied the Effra away beneath the arches of Vauxhall station. The line of the stream is aligned with the long road tunnel of South Lambeth Place—whose dark damp patches and mineral deposits percolating through the brickwork overhead give the illusion of passing through some subterranean grotto. Emerging from South Lambeth Place into the present-day Vauxhall bus station, the Wandsworth Road crosses the river here at the site of Cox's Bridge. This was the third of the medieval bridges and, like the others, the subject of much argument. As late as 1703 Lambeth Vestry had engaged in nine years of litigation with the County of Surrey over who was responsible for its upkeep.

At this point the Effra meets Bazalgette's third intercepting sewer, the Southern Low Level, which crosses the Effra at Wandsworth Road on its route from Battersea and then follows the Effra's valley, but flowing in the opposite direction, back around The Oval along the line of Harleyford Road before heading along Camberwell New Road. Beyond Cox's Bridge the Effra flows through its final stretch into the Thames.

Cox's bridge over the Effra is seen in front of the Civil War fortifications at Vauxhall, supposedly ca 1650.

This stretch was known as Vauxhall Creek, or sometimes Lambeth Creek (See Plate 4A). Until the beginning of the nineteenth century this area had been an uneasy mix of suburban villas with grounds running down to the Thames and pleasure gardens for the fee-paying public. Vauxhall Gardens to the north was the largest and most famous, but the Effra flowed out beside Cumberland Gardens, a smaller tea gardens modelled on, and less successful than, Vauxhall but with a spectacular river view (See Plate 5). The mouth of the Effra here was also the finish point for Vauxhall Gardens' sailing matches: starting at Blackfriars Bridge, the boats raced upstream to Putney, then returned to the finish line at Cumberland Gardens for the presentation of the prizes.

The construction first of Vauxhall Bridge in 1816 and then the railway into Waterloo in 1847 ended Vauxhall's aspirations as a desirable riverside address. Brunswick House, the large Georgian villa next to St George Wharf on Wandsworth Road, survives as an unusual reminder of what the area might have once been. In the late 1830s its garden ground, running down to the Thames and bordered by the Effra to the east, was acquired by Price's who needed a factory with river access for their development of stearine as a cheap raw material for candles. After centralising their operations at Battersea in the 1850s, they sold the Vauxhall site to the Phoenix Gas Company who replaced the factory with their gas holders. By the 1890s, after the storm relief sewer system was feeding into the new outfalls under Vauxhall Bridge, the creek no longer flowed into the Thames and it became a sealed off dock. When the gasworks closed in the late 1950s the creek was

Prices Candle Works at Vauxhall; the mouth of the Effra is in the foreground, 1847.

filled in and the Nine Elms Cold Store was constructed over its site after 1961. The Cold Store, providing emergency storage for meat and butter, proved short-lived and had ceased operating by the 1980s. In its dereliction the building found a new unplanned purpose as a nocturnal cruising ground for sexual encounters between the clientele of two nearby gay pubs, the Royal Vauxhall Tavern and the Market House. It was demolished and then redeveloped as St George Wharf in 2001.

Which just leaves the question of the two outfalls beneath Vauxhall Bridge. Many people believe they represent the mouth of the River Effra but this is wrong. By the eighteenth century the Effra's course had been tidied up into a single mouth that ran into the Thames through Vauxhall Creek (now an unmarked point on the river path and wall in front of the St George Wharf towers). By the time the outfalls were constructed in the early 1890s Vauxhall Creek had been sealed off, and the Effra had long since ceased to flow as a river. The outfalls are the mouths of two storm relief sewers, now called the Brixton and the Clapham Storm Relief Sewers, built to drain surface water from South London's streets after heavy rainfall. Some sections follow the course of some parts of the old river, but they bear no relation to the Effra. They will shortly disappear as part of the Thames Tideway Tunnel project when their future flow will be piped down into the new main sewer beneath the Thames.

The Nine Elms Cold Store built over Vauxhall Creek, 1978.

Clapham Storm Relief Sewer outfall beside Vauxhall Bridge, ca 1955.

THE PROBABLE COURSE OF THE PRE-MEDIEVAL RIVER

Unlike the previous walking itinerary for the main course of the Effra, which is based on firm historical evidence, it needs to be stressed that this final section following the course for the pre-medieval river is based on research that is probable but not yet completely proven. The first section of the route between Brixton Road and Walworth/Camberwell Road had disappeared before the eighteenth century, there is little evidence for it on maps and it can only be surmised. The latter section from the Walworth/Camberwell Road is based on the hypothesis that the original course of the Effra flowed into the Earl's Sluice.

One distinctive feature of its route from Kennington through to Rotherhithe is that the entire course lies below what was once known as Trinity High Water, now the 'High Water Mark of Ordinary Tides', meaning that at any point along it at high tide, the Thames will be at least six feet above the land.

From Brixton Road opposite the junction with Prima Road, where the Effra was

Albany Road from Burgess Park.

subsequently diverted west under the roadway beneath Hazard's Bridge, another stream, still visible in sections on one early nineteenth-century map, flowed north across Kennington Common/Park to curve east around what are now the tennis courts to St Agnes Place. It may then have passed across the Brandon Estate and flowed east to the junction of Walworth and Camberwell Roads close to the line of John Ruskin Street. This area was known in medieval times as Hazard's Marsh, but had been drained and become cultivable by the seventeenth century, presumably after this old course of the river had ceased to flow.

Beyond the Walworth/Camberwell Road the route becomes clearer after the Effra joined up with a stream flowing north from Denmark Hill that remained in water until the nineteenth century. This combined stream then crossed Camberwell Road just to the north of Albany Road at Boundary Lane, whose name is a reminder of the stream's other function in marking the parish and manorial boundaries of Newington and Walworth to the north and Camberwell to the south. This ancient boundary suggests that the line of the stream here must have been natural and established. At this point it was flowing to the south of Walworth Marsh, another area that had become drained by the eighteenth century and was then known as Walworth Common Fields, again suggesting the effectiveness of the new cut in drying out this marshland. Albany Road follows the gentle curve of this boundary stream, but it is a pleasanter walk along the line of the straighter old course of the Grand Surrey Canal in Burgess Park on the other, south, side of Albany Road. The canal, opened in sections from 1807, takes a straighter line to the Thames.

At the Old Kent Road the stream passed under the medieval bridge of St Thomas Watering, just to the north of the Thomas A Becket pub. Ancient bridge name and current pub name are both reminders that the Old Kent Road was the London pilgrimage route to the shrine of St Thomas at Canterbury—and this was the first point beyond London at which Canterbury pilgrims might stop to water their horses.

From the other, east, side of the Old Kent Road the stream was known as the Earl's Sluice: a name believed to derive from Robert, an illegitimate son of King Henry I, whom his father created Earl of Gloucester in 1121/2. Gloucester held the manor of Camberwell whose northern boundary was defined by the line of this sluice. Like all the streams in North Lambeth and Southwark it was a vital part of the drainage system which, along with the Thames walls, kept the lands here just above the floods and so viable for agriculture. In 1570 the Sewer Commissioners had commented that 'the Earles Sluice is in great decaye, both before the same sluice and behind it to the great danger of the whole levye'.[16]

The course of the stream now flows along Humphrey Street (the old line of Earl Road that previously crossed it is now lost under the Tesco superstore). Turn right at the roundabout on the edge of the retail park to follow Rolls Road and then Catlin Road to Rotherhithe New Road. The long institutional-looking brick wall to the left is the boundary wall of the former Bricklayers Arms depot, a failed passenger terminus that then became a large railway goods

---

16 London County Council, *Court Minutes of the Surrey and Kent Sewers Commission*, vol. 1, 1909, p. 76

yard. Housing now covers the site. The course of the sluice ran just to the south of Rolls Road, originally through Roll's Marsh, remembered as 'always under water in winter'. On eighteenth-century maps this route was shown as the 'Footway to the St Helena's', a tea gardens to which South Londoners would walk out and which remained in damp and semi-rural seclusion on the edge of Rotherhithe until late in the nineteenth century.

The view to the City from Bermondsey South station.

The Earl's Sluice passes beneath Bermondsey South station, but the converging railway lines create a natural barrier which the walker has to pick a way around. Follow the curve of Ilderton Road to the south past the travellers' site and then follow the signs to Millwall Football Club down Zampa Road under the first railway line and then turn left into Bolina Road which will wind you under another four railway arches out into the Hawkestone Estate where street names like Island Road are again a reminder that this was once low-lying and flooded marshes; St Helena Road marks the site of the tea gardens.

Follow Reculver Road into Oldfield Grove and take the footbridge over the East London line. Go left out of Trundleys Terrace and then right onto Bestwood Street, left on to Lower

[SP8] St Helena's Tea Gardens, which advertised itself as the 'Eastern Vauxhall', 1839.

Road and right onto Chilton Grove to get back onto to the line of the Earl's Sluice. The now disused but still elegant red-brick Earl Pumping Station on Chilton Grove was one of the storm relief pumping stations which, like the one at Vauxhall Creek, was used to pump surges of surface water into the Thames. Dogleg left and right out of Chilton Grove onto Plough Way, where a surviving relocated boundary marker between the counties of Kent and Surrey is another reminder that the course of this Earl's Sluice was an ancient one. This will take you east to the river and the Thames path via Helsinki Square and St George's Stairs. The surviving section of a stone bridge that used to cross the Sluice has been moved here, with its 1819 parish boundary marker between St Paul's Deptford and St Mary's Rotherhithe parishes. It was at this point before the thirteenth century that the Effra flowed into the Thames.

The wall of the Earl's Sluice bridge.

BIBLIOGRAPHY

PUBLISHED SOURCES

Aldridge, W., *The Wild Birds of Norwood*, 1885

Allen, Benjamin, *Natural History of the Mineral Waters in Great Britain*, 1691

Allen, Thomas, *History and Antiquities of the Parish of Lambeth*, 1826

Allen, Thomas, *The History and Antiquities of London, Westminster, Southwark, and Parts Adjacent*, 1837

Aubrey, John *Natural History and Antiquities of the County of Surrey*, begun in 1673

Barton, Nicholas, *The Lost Rivers of London*, 1962

Besant, Sir Walter, *London South of the Thames*, 1899

Blanch, W.H., *The Parish of Camberwell*, 1875

Brayley, Edward, *History of the County of Surrey*, vol. III, 1847

Brunton, John, *A Short History of Herne Hill*, 2011

Codrington, Thomas, 'London South of the Thames', *Surrey Archaeological Collections*, 28, 1915

Coulter, John, *Norwood Past*, 1996

Dobraszczyk, Paul, *Into the Belly of the Beast: Exploring London's Victorian Sewers*, 2009

Dixon, Ken, *Effra; Lambeth's Underground River*, 1993

English Place Names Society, *Place Names of Surrey*, English Place Names Society, vol. XI, 1969

Foord, A.S., *Springs, Streams and Spas of London*, 1910

Galer, A.M., *Norwood and Dulwich Past and Present*, 1890

Geological Survey, *The Water Supply of Surrey from Underground sources*, Memoirs of the Geological Survey, 1912

Halliday, Stephen, *The Great Stink of London: Sir Joseph Bazalgette and the Cleansing of the Victorian Capital*, 1999

Herne Hill Society, *Herne Hill Heritage Trail*, 2013

James and Malcolm *General View of the Agriculture of the County of Surrey*, 1794

London County Council, *Centenary of London's Main Drainage*, 1855-1955, 1955

London County Council, *Court Minutes of the Surrey and Kent Sewers Commission*, vol. 1, 1909

Manning, O. and Bray, W., *History and Antiquities of the County of Surrey*, 1804-14

MOLAS, *The Prehistory and Topography of Southwark and Lambeth*, MOLAS Monograph 14, 2002

Muthesius, Stefan, *The English Terraced House*, 1982

Philips, W.T., *Norwood in Days of Old*, 1912

Piper, Alan, *A History of Brixton*, 1996

Ruskin, John, *Praeterita*, vol. 1, 1884

Surrey and Kent Sewers Commission, *Reports Relating to Sewage, Sewers Surrey and Kent*, 1843
Survey of London, *St Mary Lambeth, Part I*, vol. XXIII, 1951
Survey of London, *St Mary Lambeth, Part 2*, vol. XXVI, 1956
Tames, Richard, *Dulwich and Camberwell Past: With Peckham*, 1997
Talling, Paul, *London's Lost Rivers*, 2011
Victoria County History, Surrey, 1912
Warbis, J., *River Effra*, 1979, unpublished paper (LAD)
Wilson, J.B., *The Story of Norwood*, 1973

UNPUBLISHED SOURCES

LONDON METROPOLITAN ARCHIVES

Surrey and Kent Sewers Commission: minutes, reports, plans
Metropolitan Commission of Sewers minutes, reports, plans
Metropolitan Board of Works: minutes, contracts, plans, reports
London County Council: minutes and reports

LAMBETH ARCHIVES

Lambeth Vestry minutes
Lambeth Sewers committee minutes
Enclosure, tithe, estate, Ordnance Survey, drainage and sewer maps
Household drainage applications.
Title deeds collections

THE NATIONAL ARCHIVES

Records of the Court of Kings Bench

SOME USEFUL WEBSITES

http://www.martindknight.co.uk/MKsResearch.html
Martin Knight's website is very strong on the geography and geology of the Effra

http://www.vauxhallandkennington.org.uk/effra.html
Martin Stanley's website is good on route and maps

http://www.wildlondon.org.uk/lost-effra
London Wildlife Trust's pages describe their Lost Effra project

http://landmark.lambeth.gov.uk/
Lambeth Archives website has many images of the Effra and local area

INDEX